"I love this new devotional! Julie writes straight from the heart and I am impressed with the depth of spiritual insight she conveys. Each prayer is authentic and relevant. I can't wait to buy a hundred copies to share with my family and friends! There is no lack of Christian literature and there are many devotionals, but many seem lacking in either spiritual truth or emotional honesty. Julie excels in addressing both sides of the spectrum through this relationship altering devotional. I feel blessed to know her!"

—Julie Andrews, teacher, wife and mother,
Chagrin Falls, Ohio

"What another great piece of work by my friend Julie!!! I am continuously blessed and encouraged by her faith. There are many times when I read the Word, that I simply don't know what to say to our awesome and mighty God....and Julie gives me a way to read the Psalms and do just that. I am honored to have the opportunity to preview her work and love the fact that Julie continues to share her gift with others."

—Dwight Long
Director of Men's Ministries
Hope Ministries
Des Moines, Iowa

This book is a real page turner....My plan was to read the introduction and one Psalm with prayer. Some mystery books make me feel I cannot put down the book, but with "Praying Through the Psalms" by Julie Walker Mitchell I could not stop with just one Psalm, I wanted to keep reading. Julie truly is blessed by God with the ability to express herself with just the right words. "Praying through the Psalms" draws you in and was hard for me to put down. Julie expresses what I wish I had the ability to say.

—Frances Dickenson
Dickenson Insurance Group
West Palm Beach, Florida

"I want to thank Julie for sharing her enduring faith and trust in God through her books. She has inspired me with her written devotional words in her first book, *365 Days of Hope*. I have given this book to our children and family and our friends hoping that they too will live their lives knowing that the Lord is in complete control. I am looking forward to sharing her new book, *Praying Through the Psalms* with our small group Bible Study group. Julie's words help me to hear the voice of God and trust and acknowledge Him in everything that I do."

—Jack Bolinski
Retired Dentist
The Villages, Florida

"Once again, Julie shares with us her unyielding faith in God, this time by celebrating the psalms. Her message is steadfast: That every trial and tribulation in life has meaning, but the true meaning can only be discovered if you journey through life with God at your side. I now have two Julie Mitchell books on my bedside table to comfort me as I begin and end each day."

—Jean Koehler,
Social Entrepreneur,
Detroit, MI

"I have been truly blessed as I read Julie Mitchell's first book, *365 Days of Hope* each morning. The Lord has often spoken to me through the words and the Scripture readings. I was especially inspired by the month of March dealing with the book of Proverbs. I read the devotion and the Bible…what a wealth of information on how to live my life! I sincerely enjoy reading the devotional book and have been doing so for two years. I can't wait to read the next book, *Praying Through the Psalms*."

—Merilyn Francioso
Lady Lake, Fl

"As image-bearers of our Creator God, we have a need to relate to him, to know him, to worship and enjoy him. His gift of prayer helps us to do just that—to draw near to him. In "Praying Through the Psalms," Julie Walker Mitchell has expressed the heart of the psalmist, the heart of worship, the heart that recognizes the need to commune with its Maker. Pick up this book of prayers and make them your own. Do it daily. Do it in the morning before the busyness of the day. Truth and love pour out of every page. You'll find yourself saying, along with David, 'You are my Lord; apart from you I have no good thing.'"

—Matt Mosher
Financial Analyst
Boone, NC

"Praying Through the Psalms" is a very easy read we use it each day as our morning devotional. Julie's prayers help us to put on our full armor of hope and courage, as we begin each day. The book of Psalms is a book of prayers that describe man's trials, hopes and dreams brought before his Holy God. The Psalmist reminds us of God's eternal promises and commitments and promises to us. Our trials are no different today than they were when they were originally penned by David and the other authors. Following each Psalm, Julie's thoughtful prayers help to remind us of the hope and faith that is ours through faith and trust in God. Thank you, Julie, for your friendship and for allowing us to be an early part of your new Psalms devotional!

—Richard Thompson,
Manufacturer's Rep. and Carla Thompson,
Licensed Physical Therapist,
Solon, Ohio

Using the book of Psalms as inspiration, Julie shows us how to be introspective about the intent that goes into our prayers. She reminds us, through her thoughtful choice of Bible verses and her beautiful prayers that it takes humility and practice to develop an open dialogue with God and to trust in His responses. With this book Julie gives us the tools to bring the power of prayer back into our hearts and minds.

—Tammy Simone,
Homeschool mother and wife,
Solon, Ohio

PRAYING
through the
PSALMS

God's blessings,

Janie Mitchell

PRAYING
through the
PSALMS

150 DAYS OF PRAYER

JULIE WALKER MITCHELL

TATE PUBLISHING
AND ENTERPRISES, LLC

Published by Tate Publishing & Enterprises, LLC
127 E. Trade Center Terrace | Mustang, Oklahoma 73064 USA
1.888.361.9473 | www.tatepublishing.com

Tate Publishing is committed to excellence in the publishing industry. The company reflects the philosophy established by the founders, based on Psalm 68:11,
"The Lord gave the word and great was the company of those who published it."

Published in the United States of America

ISBN: 978-1-62024-347-3
1. Religion / Christian Life / Prayer
2. Religion / Biblical Meditations / Old Testament
12.05.11

DEDICATION

This book is dedicated to all the people who have trouble pouring out their hearts in prayer. May this book help you to open the lines of communication between you and your loving Heavenly Father. I pray that this will be a starting point to building your relationship with God by praying and sharing your joys and sorrows. May your prayer time grow and develop as you read through the Psalms, and may you be blessed by spending time each day in prayer. May you draw closer to your Creator, Redeemer, and Savior and cherish the time you spend with him. May your life be changed through the power of prayer, and may your faith grow as you spend time with God. May this book be the beginning of a great adventure in your life as you commit yourself to prayer and God's Word. "All Scripture is God-breathed and is useful for teaching, rebuking, correcting and training in righteousness, so that the man of God may be thoroughly equipped for every good work" (2 Timothy 3:16-17).

This book is also dedicated to my loving family and friends who have always supported me with their love, kindness, faithfulness, and prayers. Thank you to the many people who have lifted up our family in prayer. Thanks be to God for answering our prayers and providing for our needs each day! May you be encouraged as you read through this book and draw near to our Savior and Lord. May you be blessed as you "pray through the Psalms."

To God be all glory, honor, and praise. I pray that He would be glorified through this book, in this world and throughout this life. May His Word be read and studied for it has the power to change people's lives and hearts. Our God is awesome, and He can do all things! Nothing is impossible for him! He is worthy of our thanks and praise.

ACKNOWLEDGMENTS

During difficult times in life, I have always been comforted by reading through the Psalms. David was truly a "man after God's own heart," and he very eloquently pours out his heart in prayer. He praises God during wonderful times and he questions God when times are not going as well. He seems to be in constant communication with God as he walks with Him each day. David was sinful and he made many mistakes. It is comforting to know that no person is perfect. We all need to grow and mature in our faith, and we need to continuously seek God's will for our lives. We need love and forgiveness, and we need a Savior because we can't save ourselves. We, like David, need God's mercy and grace. David prays in Psalm 51,

> Have mercy on me, O God, according to your unfailing love; according to your great compassion blot out my transgressions. Wash away all my iniquity and cleanse me from my sin. For I know my transgressions, and my sin is always before me. Create in me a pure heart, O God, and renew a steadfast spirit within me. Do not cast me from your presence or take your Holy Spirit from me. Restore to me the joy of your salvation and grant me a willing spirit, to sustain me.
>
> Psalm 51:1-3, 10-12

This book was inspired by many people, and I would like to take a moment to acknowledge some of the people who are special to me. I was so encouraged by comments and testimonies about my first book, *365 Days of Hope*. I wanted to write something to help people through difficult times and share with them the *hope* that only comes from God. His peace passes all understanding, and it is available to us if we simply ask. God loves us and wants to give us every good and perfect thing. He cherishes the time we spend with Him just as a father longs to spend time with his children. We are precious to God, and it is amazing to think that He created each of us as a precious and unique person. Sometimes we feel inadequate, sometimes we feel unworthy, sometimes we feel lost or overwhelmed, sometimes we need reassurances, and sometimes we need help just getting out of bed. This life is hard! God gives us the Bible, which is His Word to inspire us, to show us the way, and to teach us his will. He brings special people into our lives to encourage and love us. He gives us His promises, and He gives us an opportunity to talk with Him any time of the day or night. He is always there for us. He longs to draw near to us, to hold us in His arms and comfort us and listen to our prayers. He knows everything about us and He still loves us.

I would like to thank my wonderful husband of twenty-five years. We have grown and learned so much walking through this journey of life together. You have blessed my life with your love, faithfulness, encouragement, devotion, dedication, and commitment to prayer. As you begin and end each day with prayer, I can see into your heart and know what is important to you. You are an excellent father, and your life is a wonderful example of love. You give so much of yourself to others, and you deeply love your family and friends. You are strong and amazingly resilient. You are caring and compassionate, and you allow the love of God to shine through your life. You are a miracle, and I thank God for you every day!

I am thankful for our two precious daughters, Kristen and Diana. You are growing into incredible young women who are strong, beautiful, vibrant, exciting, and adorable. I am so proud of you, and the people that you have become. You have worked hard to achieve many things, and I hope and pray that you will always draw your strength, comfort, encouragement and love from God, our Father. He has blessed you with so many gifts, talents, and blessings, and I pray that you will walk with Him and talk with Him all the days of your life. You are special, and I am so thankful that God blessed my life with your presence. Kristen and Diana, I love you always and forever!

Thank you, Sally, for your consistency in my life. Your friendship, which is truly a gift from God, has been an important part of my life since my high school days. Although we went to separate colleges and lived hundreds of miles away from each other, God always kept us close in spirit, and you are truly my sister in many ways. I pray that God would bless your ministry and that you would be a shining example to the youth at our church! You have a special heart for God and for youth ministry. May God forever be your source of power, strength, faith, hope, and love! May He give you His wisdom, guidance, and strength each day as you plan and prepare activities, Bible studies, events, classes, conference, and times of fellowship and fun. You are a blessing to so many people, and I am blessed to know you!

I love my parents and their incredible support and encouragement. I know that I can count on them for anything. My dad read through my last manuscript in two weeks so he could finish before his golf trip. My mom has always been my supporter and cheerleader throughout my life and has been devoted to prayer. Although my parents live far away, I know that they would be happy to do anything I asked of them. Thank you for your unconditional love and your living example of Christian marriage and parenting. It was so exciting celebrating your fiftieth wedding anniversary! What a wonderful occasion filled with love, laughter, and joy!

A special thank you goes out to Powell Woods who is now retired and able to spend more time with the people that he loves. You have always been an inspiration. Thank you for your faithfulness in pastoring the sheep that God has entrusted to you! Thank you for your willingness to read through another one of my books. Thank you for your devotion to prayer and for keeping our family in your prayers daily! We are blessed by your friendship, your knowledge, your faithfulness, and your love. May you be blessed as you travel and pursue new and different activities. I am so proud of your new commitment to working out and getting stronger. I am so thankful for your leadership, your friendship and support! May God bless you and Karen in all that you do!

I am blessed to have so many wonderful friends. Thank you for your willingness to read through my manuscript and write comments and an endorsement for my book. It means so much to me that you would take the time in your busy schedule to write some words of encouragement. I am blessed by your friendship and thankful for your love.

Thank you to all the people at Tate Publishing for their support and for all the work that they have put into this manuscript to make it into an incredible book! Thank you to my editor, James Bare, for his creative ideas and for encouraging me to add questions for the reader each day. I hope and pray that people will "dig deeper" and grow in their faith. Thank you Shawn Collins for his work on the cover, to Nathan Harmony for his work on the interior design of this book, and to all the staff: from acquisition to editing, the layout and design group, the graphic artists, the marketing and publicity teams, and everyone who worked to make this dream into a reality. There is so much work that goes into a book, and everyone works together to turn the manuscript into a real book! Thank you for your time, your effort, your patience, your support and encouragement, and all your hard work! It is truly appreciated!

I want to thank you my readers for your support! Many of you have shared wonderful stories with me about how God has blessed you through my writing. I know that all the talent and abilities I have are gifts from God and He deserves all the glory, honor, and praise. Some of you have shared that you have breakfast with me every morning as you read through my devotional book. Others have said that my book sits on your nightstand and you end the day by reading God's Word and some encouragement and hope from me. It seems like many people have hardships and difficulties in their lives, and I hope and pray that you are encouraged by reading God's Word and drawing near to Him. He has all the answers even when we don't even know the right questions to ask. His love for us is incredible! We are blessed to walk with Him and talk with Him. I pray that you are blessed as you spend time in prayer! May this be the beginning of your journey with God, and may it grow into a beautiful relationship.

I pray that God would be glorified and honored in this work. I pray that His Word would touch your heart and your life and that you would be blessed. I know that He has given me the words to write and the prayers to be prayed. I pray that He would bless this work and bring it into the hands of those who need it most. This is my prayer for you:

> Love must be sincere. Hate what is evil; cling to what is good. Be devoted to one another in brotherly love. Honor one another above yourselves. Never be lacking in zeal, but keep your spiritual fervor, serving the Lord. Be joyful in hope, patient in affliction, faithful in prayer.
>
> Romans 12:9-12

To God be the glory now and forevermore. May you be blessed by reading this book and by spending time in prayer.

In His love,
Julie Walker Mitchell

TABLE OF CONTENTS

FOREWORD

I have known Julie Walker Mitchell for over twenty-five years as a pastor, a friend, and a fan. When I think of Julie, two things come to mind: a gifted and dedicated athlete and a deeply devout Christian. At first glance these characteristics might seem divergent—even mutually exclusive. Athletes strive to maximize human power and achievement while Christians rely upon God and trust Him completely. The former seems active, the latter passive. How can one person be both things? But as Julie has demonstrated in her life and writing, there is no conflict between the two. As an athlete Julie has excelled. She and her father have competed in National Father-Daughter tennis championships, winning four national titles. As a believer, through her and her husband Scott's prayers, the scourge of multiple myeloma which attacked him over eight years ago has been kept at bay—an outcome which is nothing short of a medical miracle. Julie is a Christian who has brought the tenacity and endurance of a professional athlete to her faith life. Through her faith, God has blessed her family in extraordinary ways.

Both Julie's Christian faith and her athletic gifts come into play in this book of prayers on the Psalms. There are two groups of people repeatedly mentioned in the Psalms: "the righteous" and "the wicked." One might be inclined to think of "the righteous" as morally upright people—those who keep God's commands—and "the wicked" as sinful people who don't. But this really makes no sense because by that standard there would be no righteous people in the world or in the Bible: everyone would be numbered among "the wicked" for "all have sinned and fall short of the glory of God." (Romans 3:23) No, in the Psalms the righteous are simply those who "call upon the name of the Lord," who strive to walk in His ways, and who trust him for forgiveness when they fail. In other words, "the righteous" are people of faith who have a relationship with God and who trust Him for all good things—for health, for forgiveness of their sins, for deliverance from their enemies, and ultimately, for salvation. "The wicked'" on the other hand, are those who have abrogated their relationship with God and who have chosen to go their own way.

What shines through all of Julie's prayers to me is the "tenacious righteousness" of a soul that doggedly perseveres in calling on the Name of the Lord, day after day, Psalm after Psalm, with a firm trust that He will protect and bless her and her family. It furnishes us with a model of Christian endeavor, a model which we would all do well to imitate.

—Powell Woods
"Soli Deo Gloria"

INTRODUCTION

The following pages are filled with prayers that have been inspired by the Psalms. King David was a "man after God's own heart" (1 Samuel 13:14), and he was the author of many of the Psalms. It is my prayer that you would read through the book of Psalms and study God's Word. These prayers are meant to inspire you and give you the words to say. Prayer is a privilege. It is our opportunity to talk to God. We can pour out our hearts and our souls. We can share our joys and our sorrows. We can confess our sins and seek forgiveness. We can pray for others and pray for ourselves.

> If my people, who are called by name, will humble themselves and pray and seek my face and turn from their wicked ways, then I will hear from heaven and will forgive their sin and will heal their land.
>
> 2 Chronicles 7:14

We can pray for wisdom and guidance. We can pray for comfort and for strength. We can pray for health and safety. We can simply talk to the Lord continuously throughout our day. Some people pray at night and some people pray in the morning. Some people pray before meals and some people only pray during times of crisis and emergencies. There is no perfect way to pray, but God encourages us to come before him in prayer.

"For I know the plans I have for you," declares the Lord, "plans to prosper you and not to harm you, plans to give you hope and a future. Then you will call upon me and come and pray to me, and I will listen to you. You will seek me and find me when you seek me with all your heart."

Jeremiah 29:11-13

Therefore let everyone who is godly pray to you while you may be found; surely when the mighty waters rise, they will not reach him. You are my hiding place; you will protect me from trouble and surround me with songs of deliverance. I will instruct you and teach you in the way you should go; I will counsel you and watch over you.

Psalm 32:6-8

The Psalms are filled with prayers, with songs of praise, and with hymns of worship. Sometimes we don't know the words to say because our hearts are heavy or filled with grief. Sometimes we cannot even begin to pray because our problems seem so difficult and answers seem to be impossible. Sometimes we are overwhelmed and we are hurting. These are the times when we need to cling to God. We need to hold on tightly as if our lives depend upon it, for sometimes they do! God wants to have a relationship with us. As we open our hearts to Him and begin to pray, we draw closer to Him. He will guide and lead us, if we only ask. If we seek Him, He will be found. He knows us better than we know ourselves. He created us and He knows our hearts. Even though we are not perfect, He still loves us more than we could possibly know or understand or even imagine. He has promised to always be with us. Nothing can separate us from His love. He has promised to never leave us or forsake us.

Prayer is our opportunity to talk to God, and I pray that you would find time each day to read His holy Word, the Bible, and draw near to Him. He is waiting with open arms to draw you close. God loves you, no matter who you are or what you have done. Journey with me through the Psalms and open your hearts to the power of prayer. As you pray through these Psalms, feel free to use your own words and pour out your hearts, your problems, your burdens, and your confessions. Take time to thank God for answers to prayers and for the wonderful blessings that He has given you. These prayers are merely a starting point to begin to build your relationship with God, our Heavenly Father. There is some space to write your own prayers and prayer requests after each day! You can make this your personal prayer journal. You can look back and see how God is working in your life and how He has answered your prayers. There are also some questions for you to ponder that will give you an opportunity to dig deeper into the meaning of the Psalm. This is also a chance for you to apply what you are reading to your life and to grow in your faith.

> I pray also that the eyes of your heart may be enlightened in order that you may know the hope to which he has called you, the riches of his glorious inheritance in the saints, and his incomparably great power for us who believe.
>
> Ephesians 1:18-19

May God bless you along this journey called "life." May your faith blossom and grow. May "the eyes of your heart" be opened, and may you know the peace of God, which passes all understanding. May God always be your source of strength, faith, hope, and love.

> Now to him who is able to do immeasurably more than all we ask or imagine, according to his power that is at work within us, to him be glory in the church and in Christ Jesus throughout all generations, for ever and ever! Amen.
>
> Ephesians 3:20-21

All Scripture Quoted in this book is taken from the NIV Bible

SECTION 1:

Psalm 1-10

Day 1

Blessed is the man who does not walk in the counsel of the wicked or stand in the way of sinners or sit in the seat of mockers. But his delight is in the law of the Lord, and on his law he meditates day and night.

Psalm 1:1-2

Dear Heavenly Father,

You have given us your precious Word: your law, your counsel, your wisdom, and your instructions. Help us to cherish Your Word and to spend time every day reading, studying, and meditating on the words You have given us in the Bible. Thank you for giving us instruction and guidance for living. You have given us everything that we need. We have the opportunity to listen to You and to seek Your guidance by spending time in Your Word. Thank you for loving us so much and for caring about every aspect of our lives. Thank you for providing for all of our needs and knowing what we need before we even ask.

You are God! You are almighty and all-powerful, all-knowing, and awesome. Let Your light and Your love shine in our hearts and lives. Help us to delight in You and in Your Word. Help us to seek You first and desire to do Your will for our lives. Thank you for loving us and for giving us blessing upon blessing. Please give us wisdom in making decisions about our lives, our friends, our careers, and our families. Help us not to be led astray by others; by those who pursue evil ways and wicked deeds. Send Your Holy Spirit to strengthen our faith and enable us to stand firm. Walk with us each day and show us Your will for our lives. Lead us along the path that we should follow. Bless us as we walk with You and help us to trust in You completely. We believe Your Word and trust in Your promises. Be our strength and our guide today and always.

In Your name we pray. Amen.

Digging Deeper:

How do you embrace God's wisdom on a daily basis?

_____

_____

_____

_____

Day 2

He is like a tree planted by streams of water, which yields its fruit in season and whose leaf does not wither. Whatever he does prospers. For the Lord watches over the way of the righteous, but the way of the wicked will perish.

Psalm 1:3, 6

Dear Heavenly Father,

Your Word feeds us each day and provides strength and power in our lives. You provide for all of our needs and take care of us each day. Help us to trust in You and cling to You. As a tree needs water for growth and to yield fruit, so we need You and Your Word to feed our souls and strengthen our faith. In You, we can do all things, and without You we are nothing. You love us, take care of us, provide for us, encourage us, build faith within us, and draw near to us. You are our Father and just as we long to provide for our children, so much more do You desire to love us, take care of us, and provide for all of our needs. You want what is best for us, and You know positively what is best for our lives. You watch over us every day and every night.

Send Your Holy Spirit to work in our lives and make us the people that You created us to be. Thank you for Your constant love and excellent care. Thank you for never giving up on us. We often disappoint You. We don't always do what we should, and we do the things that we shouldn't do. May Your Spirit keep us ever mindful of who You are and what Your will is for our lives. We ask for Your forgiveness for our sins and wrong-doings. Help us to do all things according to Your plan and not follow our selfish desires and sinful heart. We pray that You would enable us to grow and prosper by sharing our faith, building Your Kingdom, and producing fruit with eternal value. May Your will be done in heaven and on earth. May we always cling to You and find our purpose and meaning through loving and serving You.

As Your humble servants, we pray in Jesus' name. Amen.

Digging Deeper: What are you doing to produce fruit with eternal value?

_____

_____

_____

_____

Day 3

Why do the nations rage and the peoples plot in vain? The kings of the earth take their stand and the rulers gather together against the Lord and against his Anointed One.

Psalm 2:1-2

Dear Heavenly Father,

We know that You are in control of all things. You have written history, and all things and all people are under Your ultimate control. You are the same yesterday, today, and tomorrow. You are the King of kings and Lord of lords. You have created this world, and You have created each one of us. Help us to live lives worthy of our calling. Help us to seek to do Your will and spend time in Your Word.

We know that You have created the heavens and the earth. You can do all things. You have raised up leaders for us. Bless our leaders. Give them Your wisdom and guidance in making decisions. Give them the courage and strength to do what is right. Help them to discern Your will and Your way. Touch their hearts and draw them closer to You.

Help each of us to do all that we can to make this world a better place. Guide our hearts to love You first and to love our neighbors as ourselves. Help us to shine Your light in this world and to make a difference that is real and lasting. Give us boldness and courage to live the lives that You desire for us. Help us to plan and prepare each day to bring glory and honor to You and not to work in vain or oppose You in any way. Be our light and our guide in all things.

In Your holy name, we lift up these requests. Amen.

Digging Deeper: What are you doing to love God first and to love your neighbors as yourself? How do you put your faith into action?

_____

_____

_____

_____

Day 4

I will proclaim the decree of the Lord: He said to me, "You are my Son; today I have become your Father. Ask of me, and I will make the nations your inheritance, the ends of the earth your possession."

Psalm 2:7-8

Dear Heavenly Father,

Thank you for loving us. Thank you for adopting us as Your children, for calling us Your sons and daughters. Thank you for welcoming us with open arms and surrounding us with Your love and kindness. Thank you for teaching us what real love is and how to love each other. We have love because You first loved us. You created us to be in a relationship with You. You are our Father, and we are Your precious children. You have called us and drawn near to us. You have blessed us and given us the privilege of coming before You in prayer. Thank you for listening to us. Thank you for hearing our prayers.

We give You thanks and praise for who You are and who we are in You. In You, we are complete, we are made whole. Our lives are fulfilled and our joy is complete because we know You as our Father. We are designed to worship You and praise You with our lives. We need to spend time with You and to love You with our whole hearts and minds and souls, with our entire being.

Please continue to draw near to us and to minister to our needs. Please examine our hearts and make them pure. You are holy. You are God. We fall short of Your expectations, and we cannot live up to Your standard of perfection. Guide and lead us along life's way. Send Your Spirit to work in us and through us. Cleanse our hearts and purify our souls so we might draw others closer to You. Let Your love flow through our lives. Help us to be Your ambassadors here on earth.

Thank you for being our Father and for showering us with Your love. We ask all things in Jesus' name. Amen.

Digging Deeper: How do we live as a son or daughter of God on a daily basis? What things in our lives show our relationship with God on a daily basis?

Day 5

Therefore, you kings, be wise: be warned, you rulers of the earth. Serve the Lord with fear and rejoice with trembling…Blessed are all who take refuge in him.

Psalm 2:10-11, 12b

Dear Heavenly Father,

As we look at Your creation and all Your mighty works, we are filled with awe and wonder. Your creation is filled with beauty and majesty. The heavens are filled with stars beyond number and Your sun and moon light the sky by day and night. You spoke and the world was created. Your Word brought life into this world. You created all things. Your power is visible in every area of life. Help us to love You, and serve You with our whole hearts. Help us to plug into Your infinite source of power. Speak to us through Your Word, and touch our hearts and our lives. Create in us the desire to know You and love You. Help us to be the people You created us to be. Help us to seek You first in our lives and not to be selfish and self-centered. We want to do Your will for our lives. Help us to take refuge in You and trust completely in You. When we trust in ourselves, we fall short and often times we fall flat on our faces. Pick us up and carry us when we no longer know the way. Bless us with wisdom and courage to face the challenges of each new day. Send Your Holy Spirit to encourage us along life's path and show us the way we are to live. Allow us to touch the hearts of the people You have brought into our lives. Help us to serve You by serving others and love You by loving Your people. When this world seems overwhelming and we feel lost and alone, help us to see Your open arms and to seek refuge in You.

Thank you for sending Your Son to show us the true way. Thank you for creating us to be Your people and for never leaving us or forsaking us. Guide and lead us in this life's journey and help us to be a light and to shine Your love in this darkened world. In Jesus' name we pray. Amen.

Digging Deeper: What is your source of strength and comfort? Who do you turn to when you need help?

_____

_____

_____

_____

Day 6

O Lord, how many are my foes! How many rise up against me! Many are saying of me, "God will not deliver Him." But you are a shield around me, O Lord, my Glorious One, who lifts up my head.

Psalm 3:1-3

Dear Lord,

You know my life and You know everything about me. You created me, and You know my deepest thoughts and feelings. You know all things. You know my strengths and my weaknesses, my friends and my family, and my enemies and those who desire to see me fail. Sometimes this life and this world can be overwhelming. I am often surrounded by evil. This world is filled with many temptations, many who desire to see me fall and many who persecute me. Please protect me. Send Your angels to watch over me. Be my shield and protect me from my enemies. Support me and encourage me when I feel lost and alone. Draw near to me and provide for all my needs. Give me strength to face my enemies and courage to stand up for my convictions. Speak through me and allow me to shine for You. Guide my steps and lead me along Your path. Give me eyes to see the world as You see it and to love even those who persecute me. Help me to be Your hands and Your feet and to do "good" in this world for You. Help me to be an ambassador of Your love and to proclaim the good news that You have brought into this world.

Send Your Spirit to work in me and through me that I might glorify You in all things. When I am facing troubles and trials, draw near to me, and comfort me. I want to know You, to follow You, to love You, and to serve You. Thank you for being with me every step of the way. Thank you for being my Savior for saving me from myself and my sinful nature, from my enemies and their evil ways, and from a life without purpose and meaning.

I need You, Lord, and I am so thankful to have You in my life. Thank you for dying on the cross for me and for my sinfulness. Thank you for saving me in every way and loving me every day.

In Jesus' name I pray. Amen.

Digging Deeper: What does it mean to you that God is your shield? What troubles and trials are you facing now?

_____

_____

_____

_____

Day 7

To the Lord I cry aloud, and he answers me from his holy hill. I lie down and sleep; I wake again, because the Lord sustains me. I will not fear the tens of thousands drawn up against me on every side.

Psalm 3:4-6

Dear Lord,

Thank you for hearing my cries. Thank you for listening to my prayers. Thank you for promising to be with me all day and every day. Often I am afraid. Many times I doubt and seem to lose my faith in You. I try to do things my way, and I fail. I want to be in control of everything, but I am not. I want everything to go my way, but my way isn't always right. When I am selfish and self-centered, I am not seeking to please You. When I am seeking my own wants and desires, I am not looking at others and loving them. When my eyes are focused on me, I can't see the people that You have brought into my life. Open my eyes. Help me to see my selfishness as sinfulness. Help me to draw my strength and comfort from You. Forgive me when I fall short. Forgive me when I let the desires of this world crowd my life and take my eyes off You. Help me to love You first and love the people around me. When my life is in proper perspective, I am able to do Your will for my life. When the world is crashing down all around me, help me not to panic, but to see You and seek You. Help me not to be afraid of what I don't know. Help me to trust in You with my whole heart and allow You to work in my life.

I know that You can do all things. I know that You are in control and You are powerful. Calm my heart and help me to see You and not be afraid. Thank you for listening to my cries and my prayers. Thank you for being patient with me and for teaching me to love.

In Jesus' name I pray. Amen.

Digging Deeper: What do you fear the most? What selfish desires do you have that take your eyes off of God?

_____

_____

_____

_____

Day 8

Arise, O Lord! Deliver me, O my God! From the Lord comes deliverance. May your blessing be on your people.

Psalm 3:7a-8

Dear God,

Thank you for delivering me from my enemies and filling my life with Your blessings. Thank you for guiding my path and showing me Your ways. I am truly lost without You. Without You, I am nothing and I can do nothing. You are almighty, and You can do all things. You are powerful and strong, perfect and holy, gracious and loving, kind and forgiving. You are perfect, and I know that I am not. I am weak and often I am lazy. I seek the easy road instead of walking along the path that You have chosen for me. I am self-centered and easily distracted by things of this world. I can't make it on my own. I am lost without Your guidance and leadership. I am easily discouraged and sidetracked. Send Your Spirit to show me the way and teach me Your will. Remind me of Your Word and Your promises. Speak to my heart, and make my desires more like Your desires. Build me up and strengthen my faith so I might walk with You and talk with You each day. Help me to be a blessing to those around me, and to reach out in faith. Thank you for filling my life with Your blessings and for allowing those blessings to be poured out into the lives of others. You are a mighty God, and You could proclaim Your

Word through any means. Thank you for calling me and allowing me to love You and serve You. Continue to work in my life and make me the person that You created me to be. Thank you for delivering me from despair and lifting me out of the pit. Thank you for touching my heart and drawing near to me. Thank you for loving me in spite of my flaws and for washing away my sins. Create in me a new heart and a clean heart, one that desires to be more like You.

In Your name I pray. Amen.

Digging Deeper: What is one distraction that you could eliminate from your life to spend more time focused on your spiritual well-being? What would losing that thing mean to your overall quality of life?

_____

_____

_____

_____

Day 9

Answer me when I call to you, O my righteous God. Give me relief from my distress; be merciful to me and hear my prayer.

Psalm 4:1

Dear God,

Sometimes I don't even know the words to pray, but I know that You are always there ready to listen and to answer my prayers. You hear my silent cries, and You know the desires of my heart. You know everything there is to know about me, and You still love me. Thank you for creating me to be Your special child. I know that I don't always do what I should do, and I do things that I shouldn't. My thoughts are not pure and my motives are often selfish. But my true desire is to know You and to love You with my entire life, every essence of my being. I need Your tender mercy every day. I need the forgiveness that only You can give. I need to begin each day with You. I want to spend time with You and draw near to You, but sometimes the craziness and busyness of this world takes over. I get distracted from what is real and true and eternally important. I lose my perspective and my life is out of balance. You provide stability and constancy. You are my rock and my fortress. You are my strength and my shield. Help me to keep my eyes focused on You, the author and perfecter of my faith. You are righteous. You are holy. You are loving, kind, and truly amazing. Only You are worthy of our love and praise. You provide for my needs as a loving Heavenly Father. You know what is best for me. Help me to trust in You completely today and always.

Thank you for lovingly caring for me as a father would take care of his child. Thank you for blessing me; although I am not worthy of Your love and compassion, I am thankful for Your mercy and grace. Thank you for making a difference in my life. Teach me to love others as You have loved me.

In the name of Jesus, my Savior and Lord, I pray. Amen.

Digging Deeper: In what ways does God take care of you? What does it mean to you to have a Heavenly Father?

_____

_____

_____

_____

Day 10

How long, O men, will you turn my glory into shame?
How long will you love delusions and seek false gods?
Know that the Lord has set apart the godly for himself;
the Lord will hear when I call to him.

Psalm 4:2-3

Dear Heavenly Father,

This world is evil and filled with wicked people who do not know You or follow You. There are so many people who want to lead us astray and turn us away from You. Satan is the father of lies, and he wants to deceive us. He wants to take our eyes off You and make our lives ineffective. He wants us to feel empty and lonely, guilty and unworthy, powerless and small. He wants to distract us from our relationship with You and tempt us in any and every way. He wants us to question and to doubt our faith. He brings things and people into our lives to tear apart our relationship with You and steal our time with You. Help us to hear Your still, small voice. Help us to distinguish between good and evil. Guide us in the way everlasting. Enable us to hear the voice of our shepherd and to follow the path that leads to You. Send Your Holy Spirit into our lives to remind us of Your Word, Your will, and Your desires. Give us strength to overcome the evil one and the wickedness of this world. Be our shepherd and gently, lovingly, carefully lead us through each day. Help us to tune out the distractions of this world that take our focus off You.

Help us to resist the devil and his evil plans. Give us strength and courage for each day. Forgive us when we fall away and draw us into Your loving arms.

Thank you for the blessings and privileges of being Your children. Thank you for listening to our prayers. In Jesus' name we humbly ask. Amen.

Digging Deeper: What are some "false gods" or idols or distractions that get in the way of your relationship with the one, true God?

_____

_____

_____

_____

Day 11

In your anger do not sin; when you are on your beds, search your hearts and be silent. Offer right sacrifices and trust in the Lord.

Psalm 4:4-5

Dear Lord,

When we are angry, we can't always see straight. We are so caught up in what is happening in our lives. We know that we are "right," we know that we have been hurt, we want someone to pay, and we want vengeance. Teach us to forgive and to love as You have loved and forgiven us. Forgiveness isn't easy for us. We think that we deserve to be repaid and restored. We harbor resentments and carry grudges. We don't realize that we are only hurting ourselves. Anger and sinfulness fill our thoughts and our minds. They draw us away from You. Help us to remember that we often fall short of Your standard of perfection. We do what we shouldn't and don't do the things that we should. We are selfish and evil fills our hearts. We need to be forgiven every day for our shortcomings. We need to be renewed by Your love. We need to be reminded of whom we are in You and that our relationship with You is a gift. As Christians, we aren't perfect, but we have forgiveness when we ask. Search our hearts and shine Your light into areas of darkness. Fill our lives with Your love and take away our pride, our anger, our sinful ways. Let us be beacons of

Your true light and love. Let us bring kindness, love, and forgiveness into this world. Please carry our burdens and replace resentment and anger with encouragement and hope. Be patient with us and teach us how to love and trust in You completely.

In Jesus' name we humbly lift up these requests. Amen.

Digging Deeper: Who has hurt you that you need to forgive? Is there someone in your life that you have hurt and from whom you need to seek forgiveness?

Day 12

Many are asking, "Who can show us any good?" Let the light of your face shine upon us, O Lord. You have filled my heart with greater joy than when their grain and new wine abound. I will lie down and sleep in peace, for you alone, O Lord, make me dwell in safety.

Psalm 4:6-8

Dear Lord,

Let Your light shine upon us dear Lord. Bring light into the darkness, and show us Your way. We know that in You our lives are made complete. You fill us with Your light and love, Your hope and joy. In You alone we have peace. You are the only "good" in our lives. Thank you for touching our hearts and changing our lives. Thank you for sending Your Holy Spirit to live in our hearts and draw us closer to You. Thank you for giving us Your Word and for teaching us along the way. We need You to light our way and show us how to live.

When we try to do everything our way, we often fail. When things get really tough and we can't go on, we know that You can help us, guide us, and lead us. When we fail, we know You will be there to pick us up and carry us. When we are weak, You are strong. When we are lost, You guide us along the path. When our future looks dark and bleak, You provide the light and hope. You provide for the plants, the vines, and the harvest. You have made the sun to shine, the rain to fall, and the crops to grow. Help us to trust in You.

Send Your Spirit to work in our lives and help us to grow in our faith and in our love. Teach us to trust in You and to always seek You first! You fill our lives with peace and joy. Thank you for Your patience, Your love, and Your kindness. We love You! Thank you for loving us. In Jesus' precious name, we pray. Amen.

Digging Deeper: When was there a time where God carried you through a challenging period? How did you use his strength to fortify your life, emotionally and spiritually?

_____

_____

_____

_____

Day 13

Give ear to my words, O Lord, consider my sighing. Listen to my cry for help, my King and my God, for to you I pray. Morning by morning, O Lord, you hear my voice; morning by morning I lay my requests before you and wait in expectation.

Psalm 5:1-3

Dear Heavenly Father,

You promised to listen to our prayers each and every day. You promised to never leave us or forsake us. You called us to be Your children, and You promised to love us as our Heavenly Father. You know what is best for us. You answer our prayers in the best possible way. It may not always be the answer we are seeking. It may not be what we want to hear. You know what is best for us. Your wisdom is greater than ours, and Your thoughts are above ours. You know us better than we know ourselves. The answers You give to us always come in Your perfect timing, not necessarily in our time of crying or sighing. Each morning we come to You, and each morning You are there to listen to our requests and answer our prayers. We submit all things to You, and we submit our entire lives to You. We desire that Your will be done and not ours. We ask all things in Your name because we are not worthy of coming before You on our own and we do not deserve anything. We come before You humbly, knowing that we are sinful and You are holy. In this life, we struggle and You have triumphed. We are human, and You are divine. We are broken, and You are perfect and complete. In all things, in heaven and on earth, You reign. You are eternal and we are finite. May all things be done according to Your perfect plan and Your divine will. May we draw near to You and allow You to work in us to make us more like You.

Thank you for being the King of kings and Lord of lords. Thank you for listening to our prayers and our requests every morning, every evening, and throughout our days. Help us to trust in Your goodness and Your plan. In Your name we lay our requests before You and humbly pray. Amen.

Digging Deeper: How do you think that God answers your prayers? In what specific ways has He answered your cries for help?

_____

_____

_____

_____

Day 14

But I, by your great mercy, will come into your house;
in reverence will I bow down toward your holy temple.
Lead me, O Lord, in your righteousness because of my
enemies—make straight your way before me.

Psalm 5:7-8

Dear Merciful, Loving Lord,

You have blessed us beyond measure with Your mercy and Your grace. We deserve so little, yet You have given us so much. We are sinful and evil, our hearts are not pure, our motives are selfish; yet You love us in spite of ourselves. We deserve to be punished for our sinful ways, but You have chosen forgiveness. You paid the price for our sins; You suffered and died so that we might live. We are humbled because You have taken our place and paid the debt that we owed. You were humiliated, beaten, abused, scorned, whipped, punished, and hung on the cross. You endured the shame and the suffering not because of Your guilt, simply out of Your love for us. We deserve to die because we are sinful and guilty. You are perfect and sinless, holy and unblemished. We can come to the Father and have a relationship with Him because of Your blood. Through Your life and Your death, You have bridged the gap that sin has created between a Holy Father and His children. You stepped in and carried our burden and our shame. We bow down in humble adoration to You. We come before You with praise and thanksgiving for all that

You have done and all that You are. Thank you for leaving the glory and splendor of heaven to live on this earth and show us the way. Guide us along life's path today and always. Thank you for paying the price for our sins. Thank you for suffering and dying so that we might live and have eternal life. Thank you for showing us a love that is real and unconditional, one that is without limits or bounds. Thank you for taking our place and for showing us mercy and grace.

We humbly bow before You and worship and praise You. In Jesus' precious name, we pray. Amen.

Digging Deeper: How do you give thanks to God? What are the blessings for which you are most thankful?

_____

_____

_____

_____

Day 15

But let all who take refuge in you be glad; let them ever sing for joy. Spread your protection over them that those who love Your name may rejoice in you. For surely, O Lord, you bless the righteous; you surround them with Your favor as with a shield.

Psalm 5:11-12

Dear Heavenly Father,

You are our source of strength. You are our rock when the things of this world come crashing down around us. You are unchangeable, consistent, steady, completely trustworthy, and reliable. You are the same yesterday, today, and tomorrow. We need You and Your constant source of love and strength.

Surround us with Your love. Fill us with Your goodness. Strengthen our faith and guide and lead us every step of the way. When we are hopelessly lost, shine Your light into our lives and show us the way. When we are fearful and anxious, let us take refuge in You and give You our burdens to carry. When we are hurting, heal our pain and wrap Your loving arms around us. When we are mourning, comfort us and give us the courage and strength to face each new day. When we feel like we are all alone, help us to remember that You love us and we are special to You.

Continue to bless us every day so we might be a blessing to others. Be our shield when we are bombarded with life's problems and worries. Protect us from harm and keep us safe in Your loving arms. We ask all this in the name of Jesus, Your Son and our Savior. Amen.

Digging Deeper: From what do you need to be protected? What are the problems or worries in your life that are bombarding you?

_____

_____

_____

_____

Day 16

O Lord, do not rebuke me in your anger or discipline me in your wrath. Be merciful to me, Lord, for I am faint; O Lord, heal me, for my bones are in agony.

Psalm 6:1-2

Dear Lord and Savior,

Thank you for Your mercy, kindness, and love. Thank you for Your grace and for the privilege of coming before You. Thank you for listening to my prayers and for answering them with Your perfect wisdom. You know all things and You can do all things. I am weak and I make bad choices. I deserve Your punishment and even death for my sins. My ways are not Your ways, and my heart does not desire the will of Your heart. I am selfish. I am evil. I am sinful. I deserve Your anger, Your wrath, and Your discipline. I am responsible for my actions. Often times, I am tempted and I don't resist. I am hurting myself and others because of my sinful ways. I am not living my life to bring glory and honor to Your name. I am seeking my own good and my own pleasure. I confess my sins to You, O Lord. Please forgive me.

Help me to be more like You and to desire Your best for me. Help me to be the person that You created me to be. You are mighty and can do all things. Change my heart and draw close to me. Teach me Your will and Your ways, O Lord. Save me from myself and from the temptation of the evil one. Be my rock and my Savior. Be the Lord of my life. Look upon me with mercy and shower me with Your grace, not because I deserve it, but out of Your tender mercies and loving-kindness. Thank you for dying on the cross for me and for my sins. Thank you for paying the price for my mistakes and my evil desires. Help me to always seek You first and desire to follow You day by day.

Cleanse my heart and make it right with You. In Your precious name, we pray, dear Lord. Amen.

Digging Deeper: What is God calling you to do to enable you to better reflect His image? How do you approach the challenges that God lays before you?

_____

_____

_____

_____

Day 17

My soul is in anguish. How long, O Lord, how long? Turn, O Lord, and deliver me; save me because of your unfailing love. I am worn out from groaning; all night long I flood my bed with weeping and drench my couch with tears.

Psalm 6:3-4, 6

Dear Heavenly Father,

Teach us to wait on You and be patient. We want everything on our time schedule. We want it all now. We need to spend time with You in prayer. We should spend time reading Your Word. We need to walk with You and talk with You. We need to trust You. We want things done our way, and we want them done now!

You are timeless. You are infinite without beginning or end. You were before time began, and You are without end. You are the Alpha and the Omega, the beginning and the end. One day is like a thousand years to You, O Lord, and a thousand years is like a day. We wear ourselves out groaning and pleading with You. We are in anguish and in agony. We see only the here and now, whereas You see all of eternity. You know our beginning, our life span, and the day we will be with You in eternity. You have eternal vision and You see what is really important. Help us to see people and love people as You do. Help us to look through Your eyes and see our problems as an opportunity to draw closer to You. Our prayer time is special, and it is truly better to spend time with You than to worry and be tormented. "Better is one day in Your courts, than a thousand else-where" (Psalm 84:10). The relationship that is built and the time that is spent with You is infinitely more important than the answers to the prayer.

You want what is best for us, Your children. You want a relation-ship with us. Help us to begin and end every day with prayer and to treasure the time in Your presence. In Your name, O Lord, we pray. Amen.

Digging Deeper: Is there anything in your life that has caused anguish to your soul? Have you ever been worn out by groaning or weeping?

_____

_____

_____

_____

Day 18

> Away from me, all you who do evil, for the Lord has heard my weeping. The Lord has heard my cry for mercy; the Lord accepts my prayer. May all my enemies be ashamed and dismayed; may they turn back in sudden disgrace.
>
> Psalm 6:8-10

Dear Lord,

In this world we will have many problems. We will face temptation, and we will have trials. We have very real enemies who are out to destroy us. There is evil all around us. We need help. We need to be rescued. We need to be protected.

Thank you, Lord, for hearing our prayers and listening to our cries for mercy. Guard us from the evil one and from all who seek to turn us away from You. Draw near to us, and guide and lead us. Be our strength and shield. Help us to resist temptation. Teach us Your Word and Your ways, O Lord. Direct our paths. We desire to do Your will and to glorify and honor You. We don't want the evil one to prosper, and we don't want our enemies to conquer us or our spirit. Send Your Holy Spirit to guard our hearts. Allow Him to comfort and reassure us. Enable us to walk away and resist the advances of our enemies. Help us to keep our eyes focused on You.

We know that in this world there is much evil, but You have overcome this world. You have conquered sin, death, and the devil. In You, we have hope and we have life. In You, we have love and forgiveness. In You, we have comfort and strength. We can do all things through You. Thank you for hearing our prayers. In the name of Jesus, we pray. Amen.

Digging Deeper: Who are your enemies? How do you feel about them? Do you pray for them? Can you love them and forgive them?

_____

_____

_____

_____

Day 19

O Lord my God, I take refuge in you ; save and deliver me from all who pursue me. Arise, O Lord, in our anger; rise up against the rage of my enemies. Awake, my God, decree justice.

Psalm 7:1, 6

Dear God,

You are our loving Heavenly Father. You are also righteous and holy. You hate sin and evil. You are just and fair. Sinfulness must be punished. We are responsible for our lives, our thoughts and our actions. We can never live up to Your perfect standard, Your holiness. We fall short in all ways and at all times. Even when we try to do "good," our motives and our desires may not be pure. We don't always take advantage of the opportunities we have to love and serve You. We are imperfect vessels that are cracked and broken. We need to be fixed and to be made whole. We can only be complete when we are in a relationship with You.

You love us, but You hate our sinful nature. We are guilty, and we deserve to be punished. Thank you for having compassion on us and mercifully providing for our needs. Thank you for sending Your one and only Son to us, to make atonement for our sins by dying on the cross for us! Our relationship with You has been repaired and rebuilt by the blood of Your Son. Jesus did what we could never do. He lived a perfect life and died a perfect death so we could be saved. In

Christ, we are seen as perfect and our sins are forgiven. Not because of who we are, only because of what Jesus did for us are we forgiven and able to stand before You. You are our Savior and You are a righteous judge. Only by mercy are we saved and delivered from evil and our enemies.

Thank you for providing a way for us and delivering us. Thank you, Jesus, for being our Savior. In Your name we pray. Amen.

Digging Deeper: What makes you feel guilty? How does guilt affect your relationship with God?

_____

_____

_____

_____

Day 20

O righteous God, who searches minds and hearts, bring to an end the violence of the wicked and make the righteous secure. My shield is God Most High, who saves the upright in heart. I will give thanks to the Lord because of his righteousness and will sing praise to the name of the Lord Most High.

Psalm 7:9-10, 17

Dear Lord Most High,

You have created all things. You know everything there is to know about us. You know our hearts and minds. You know our wants and desires. You know our dreams, goals, and aspirations. You understand us and every aspect of our lives. You have lived in this world, and You know the trials and temptations we face. You are compassionate and loving. You are perfect! Save us from ourselves and our evil ways. Fill our hearts with Your love and mercy. Help us to share Your love with others and encourage them. Be a light unto our path so that we can lead others to Your light. We want our lives to be a reflection of Your love. We want people to notice the difference in our lives, the difference is You! You love us, and You have saved us. You have called us to be Your people, and You have blessed us to be a blessing to others. You are the Lord of lords, almighty, all-powerful, omniscient, holy and righteous, compassionate, and full of grace and truth.

Protect us from all evil and be our strength and shield. We praise You for Your abundant blessings. We thank You for who You are and for how You are working in our lives. Thank you for never giving up on us and being patient with us. Thank you for being our Savior and Lord. In Your holy name, we pray. Amen.

Digging Deeper: How do you reflect God's love in your daily life? How do you share God's love with those around you?

_____

_____

_____

_____

Day 21

O Lord, our Lord, how majestic is your name in all the earth!
You have set your glory above the heavens. When I consider
your heavens, the work of your fingers, the moon and the star
which you have set in place, what is man that you are mindful
of him, the son of man that you care for him?

Psalm 8:1, 3-4

Dear Lord,

As we look around at the beauty and splendor of this world, we
are awed. As we look to the heavens and their glory, we are amazed.
Your creation is marvelous, Your world incredible. You set each star
in its place. You created each bird, every plant, every animal, and
every person. Your power is unbelievable. You are an awesome God.
You spoke and the world came into being. You breathed life into
each one of us. You are the Creator, and we are Your creation. Who
are we that You should care about us? Who are we that You should
be mindful of our thoughts and our needs? Who are we that You
should love us? You are all-powerful and almighty, and we are a mere
part of Your world.

As we look out over the ocean and watch the waves crashing to
the shore, we get a sense of Your mighty power. As we gaze at the
stars in the sky, we know that there is order and purpose in Your
world and Your creation. You did not merely make us and leave us
on our own. You love us and care about every part of our lives. We

can have a relationship with You. You desire to spend time with us. We are special to You. You have given us meaning and purpose in life. We come before You reverently filled with awe and wonder. How majestic is Your name, O Lord. In You, we pray. Amen.

Digging Deeper: How do you recognize the gifts of God's creations? How does awareness of these gifts change your spiritual life?

_____

_____

_____

_____

Day 22

You made him ruler over the works of your hands; you put everything under his feet: all flocks and herds, and the beasts of the field, the birds of the air, and the fish of the sea, all that swim in the paths of the seas. O Lord, our Lord, how majestic is your name in all the earth!

Psalm 8: 6-9

Dear Heavenly Father,

Thank you for all of Your creation. We praise You for this beautiful world that You have given us. You have created man to watch over this world and Your creation. You have given us a great responsibility to take care of all that You have made. We have not always done a good job of caring for this world. We don't live in harmony with Your people, Your creation, Your world, or You. We tend to abuse the power that You have blessed us with, and we seek to do all things for our own good. We are selfish, and we don't look at the big picture. You see all of time and how our actions affect generations to come. Help us to be good stewards of all that we have been given. We know that everything we have comes from You. You are the giver of every good and perfect gift. We need Your wisdom and guidance to make good decisions about our lives, Your people and this world. We praise You for Your abundant blessings and the many gifts You have given to us.

Father, Your world is incredible, and Your creation is amazing. You are awesome, and Your name is greatly to be praised. You are majestic and holy, truly excellent and awe-inspiring. We are amazed by Your power and Your creation! We bow down before You, and we are humbled in Your presence. Thank you for loving us and creating us. In Your majestic name, we pray. Amen.

Digging Deeper: What words do you use to describe God's creative nature? Name some of God's creations that fill you with awe and wonder.

_____

_____

_____

_____

Day 23

I will praise you, O Lord, with all my heart; I will tell of all
your wonders, I will be glad and rejoice in you ; I will sing
praise to your name, O Most High.

Psalm 9:1-2

Dear Lord,

I will praise You with all my heart. I will praise You with my
thoughts, my words, my actions, and my life. I will praise You at all
times and all situations. Help me to praise You in all circumstances.
Sometimes, it is easier to praise Your name when things are going
well. It is easy to have a good attitude when life is good and when
all things are going according to plan. Help me to always have an
attitude of praise and thanksgiving.

I want to be a good ambassador for You. I want to shine Your
light in this world of darkness. I want to share Your Word and
tell others of Your great works. I want to share the precious gifts
and blessings that You have given to me. I know that I am blessed
because of You, because of all that You have done for me. In You, I
can do all things and be the person that You have created me to be.
I want to be a good witness even when times are hard and the road
is tough. It is during those times that people can see the evidence
of my faith and my ability to cope with trouble and trials. During
the hard times, I can show that my strength comes from You alone.

I want to always rejoice in You and praise Your holy name. Thank you for Your unconditional love and acceptance. Thank you for loving me each and every day. Help me to reach out in love to those around me. I ask all these things in the name of Jesus, my Lord and Savior. Amen.

Digging Deeper: Why is it difficult to share our faith with others? Why is it frightening to share what is so important to you? What are some ways that you can praise God with your whole heart?

_____

_____

_____

_____

Day 24

My enemies turn back; they stumble and perish before You. For you have upheld my right and my cause; you have sat on your throne, judging righteously. You have rebuked the nations and destroyed the wicked; you have blotted out their name for ever and ever.

Psalm 9:3-5

Dear Lord,

We have so many enemies. There are so many people who persecute us and desire to see us fail. The world seems to tear us down and drag us away from You. Guard us from the evil of this world. Help us to view the problems of this world as being temporary. Our relationship with You is eternal. You have overcome the world and defeated sin, death and the devil. In You, we have power and strength. You are righteous and holy. You will sit on the throne for all eternity. You are our judge. You will judge all people according to their lives. The wicked will perish and spend eternity apart from You. The righteous will live in heaven…in paradise and praise Your name throughout time. You are ultimately in control of all things! We need to give control of our lives to You!

Although we face difficult days and times, help us to keep our eyes focused on You and know that You can do all things. You are victorious, and Your name will be praised forever. One day every knee will bow and every tongue will confess that You are Lord! Help us to praise You today with our lives and with our whole hearts. Guide and lead us every day and show us Your will for our lives. Let us rejoice in the truth and not be pulled down into the pit of this world. Guard us from evil and send Your Spirit to encourage us and strengthen our faith. We humbly come before You in prayer. We praise Your name and give You thanks. In Your holy and righteous name, we pray. Amen.

Digging Deeper: What is God's role as judge? When He examines your life, will He find you innocent or guilty? Why?

_____

_____

_____

_____

Day 25

The Lord reigns forever; he has established his throne for judgment. He will judge the world in righteousness; he will govern the peoples with justice. The Lord is a refuge for the oppressed, a stronghold in times of trouble.

Psalm 9:7-9

Dear Heavenly Father,

Some people view You only as a God of love, thinking of You as our Heavenly Father who loves each of us as His precious child. People only look at one aspect of Your character and think that You will love and accept us no matter what we do or how we act. It is true that You are love, but You are also holy and righteous. Sometimes we need to accept responsibility for our thoughts, words, and deeds. We need to seek forgiveness and confess our sins. You have provided forgiveness through Your Son, Jesus Christ, and His death on the cross. He paid the price for our sins. You are just, and You will fairly judge this world. The wicked will be punished, and those who cling to You will be saved. You provide strength for the weary and hope for the oppressed. You provide abundantly for all Your children, and You know what we need before we even ask! Sometimes, Your gifts are not what we ask for but are what we truly need.

We come before You in prayer and ask for Your wisdom and guidance. You know what is best for us, and You have promised to provide for us. Your love for Your children is unconditional. We need to seek You and draw near to You. We cannot approach a holy God on our own merit. We come before You in Jesus' name, asking that You see us clothed in His righteousness and not our own sinfulness. His sacrifice was necessary to restore our relationship with You. Thank you for Your love and for providing for our every need today and always. You are Almighty and holy, just, loving and forgiving. You are everything that we truly need, want, and desire. Help us to love others as You do. We ask for forgiveness and pray all this in the name of Your Son, our Lord. Amen.

Digging Deeper: What does it mean to fear and to love God? How do you show reverence for your Heavenly Father?

_____

_____

_____

_____

Day 26

Those who know Your name will trust in you, for you, Lord, have never forsaken those who seek you. Sing praises to the Lord enthroned in Zion; proclaim among the nations what he has done.

Psalm 9:10-11

Dear Lord,

Thank you for the privilege of calling upon Your name. Thank you for allowing us to come before You in prayer. We praise and thank you for Your promise to never leave us or forsake us. We humbly bow down before You and thank you for loving us, for listening to our prayers, for forgiving us, and for caring for us. You have changed our lives forever. You have transformed us from the inside out. You have cleaned out the ugliness, selfishness, and evil within our hearts and replaced them with Your love and kindness. You took away the evil desires within our hearts and filled them with love. You have taken away the emptiness we experience and given our lives meaning and purpose in You. Since You have promised to always be with us, we are never alone. You are always available to us in every way.

We praise You for Your goodness. We thank you for Your redeeming work on the cross and for cleansing our hearts. Guide and lead us every day. Show us Your will for our lives. Help us to sing praises to Your name and proclaim Your Word among the nations. Help us to be Your ambassadors in this world and represent You to all people everywhere. Great and mighty is the Lord and worthy to be praised now and forevermore. Thank you, Lord, for all that You have done, all that You are doing, and all that You will continue to do in our lives. You have changed us, and we praise You for Your goodness. In the name of our Lord and Savior, we pray. Amen.

Digging Deeper: What does being an ambassador for God mean to you?

_____

_____

_____

_____

Day 27

But the needy will not always be forgotten, nor the hope of the afflicted ever perish. Arise, O Lord, let not man triumph; let the nations be judged in your presence. Strike them with terror, O Lord; let the nations know they are but men.

Psalm 9:18-20

Dear Lord,

You provide for us daily. You love us beyond measure. You give to us completely and love us unconditionally. You deserve all glory and praise. You are worthy of honor and admiration. You are the King of kings and Lord of lords. There is no one that is greater than You. There is no one who is worthy but You. You have conquered all our enemies. You are in control of all things and all people and all nations. You rule the heavens and the earth. You are God.

We are human. We are weak. We are needy. We are afflicted and persecuted. Others seek to destroy us and to take our eyes off You. The world wants to take away our hope and fill us with despair. The evil one wants to ruin our relationship with You by causing us to sin and fall away from our faith. We must remember that You have overcome the world. You have defeated sin, death, and the devil. You are our source of power and strength. You are the ruler of nations and the judge of all. You will not let the wicked triumph; they will suffer throughout eternity. Only Your children, who love You and who put their trust in You, will have eternal life. The ways of this world are not Your ways. Guide us and teach us Your ways and Your will for our lives. Lead us along the path of everlasting life. In Your precious name, we pray. Amen.

Digging Deeper: How do you feel when you see wicked men prosper and succeed? What gives you hope?

_____

_____

_____

_____

Day 28

Why, O Lord, do you stand far off? Why do you hide yourself in times of trouble? In his pride the wicked does not seek him; in all his thoughts there is no room for God.

Psalm 10:1, 4

Dear Heavenly Father,

We know that You love us and You created each of us to be Your precious children. You long to spend time with us and to be involved in our lives. You are always available with Your arms open wide to comfort us and draw near to us.

We are the ones who push You away. We are the ones who want to take control and do everything on our own. We are the ones who are plagued by sin that separates us from You. We know in our heads that You are always available and willing to love and forgive us. But in our hearts, we are sinful. We feel guilty. We know that we can't come before a holy God because of the evil we harbor in our lives. Our pride and our wickedness keep us from coming to You.

But we know that we aren't in control. We can't do all things. We usually fail miserably on our own. We need You! You are almighty and all-powerful. In You, dear God, we can do all things. Help us to turn away from our sinful ways and repent of the evil that fills our hearts and our lives. Help us to see clearly that You are steadfast and Your love is unfailing. You will never turn Your back on us or hide

Yourself from us. You are always ready, willing, and able to see us through every situation in our lives. You understand our weaknesses and temptations. Help us to flee from evil and draw close to You. We ask these requests in the name of Jesus, our Savior. Amen.

Digging Deeper: When does God seem far off to you, and when does He seem close? What part do you play in drawing nearer to or farther from God?

_____

_____

_____

_____

Day 29

Why does the wicked man revile God? Why does he say to himself, "He won't call me to account?" But you, O God, do see trouble and grief; you consider it to take it in hand. The victim commits himself to you; you are the helper of the fatherless.

Psalm 10:13-14

Dear God,

Sometimes it seems like the wicked prosper in this world. They have no regard for other people or even for You. They make up their own rules and do whatever is best for them. They trample people to get ahead. They have no fear of any consequences for their actions. They are committed only to themselves and their welfare. The evil man relies on his own wisdom and strength to get ahead. He delights only in himself and his gain.

Father, You have blessed us and given us every good and perfect gift. You have drawn near to us to comfort us and given us strength for each day. You have promised to be with us every step of the way. You care about all of Your creation. You love the rich and the poor, the strong and the weak, the healthy and the sick, the widows and the orphans, the families, the homeless, and all people. You want everyone to know You as their Heavenly Father. You want all people to come to You and lay down their burdens. You want to fill our lives with Your love, joy, and peace. You want to give us hope in this world and for the future.

Help us to resist evil and not be caught in the trap of wickedness. Help us to show others Your love and kindness. Send Your Holy Spirit to live in us and work through us today and always. Let us reach out to those in need and consider how we can help them by being Your arms, Your legs, Your eyes and ears, and living our lives as Your ambassadors in this world. True *joy* comes from having a proper perspective: *Jesus* first, then the needs of *others*, then *you* which is us and our own personal needs. Help us to keep this life in perspective. Each person will ultimately be accountable to You. Let us not seek vengeance but seek to love others as You do.

In the name of Your Son, we pray. Amen.

Digging Deeper: What brings you true joy? What would change in your life if you truly put Jesus first?

_____

_____

_____

_____

Day 30

The Lord is King for ever and ever; the nations will perish from his land. You hear, O Lord, the desire of the afflicted; you encourage them and you listen to their cry, defending the fatherless and the oppressed, in order that man, who is of the earth, may terrify no more.

Psalm 10:16-18

Dear Lord,

We know that You are the King of kings and Lord of lords. You are the Alpha and the Omega, the beginning and the end. You are our Creator and our Redeemer. You made each of us Your precious child. You hear our whispers, our cries, our groans, our weeping, our songs, our praise, our words, our thoughts, our sighs, our complaints, our laughter, our giggles, our yearnings, and all our prayers. Before a word is formed and spoken by our mouths, You know it. Before the song rises from our hearts, You hear it. Before the request is made, You know the best possible answer for us.

You are awesome and mighty. You shoulder all our burdens, our grief, and our sorrows. You can carry all of our loads. You have taken our sins upon You and paid for every one of them. You died for us. You have taken our place. You defend us and guide us, comfort us and sustain us. You are everything to us!

We can come before our Heavenly Father without trembling and fear. We can pray to a Holy God because You have covered our sins in Your blood. We are forgiven and loved. We will never perish. Nations will rise and fall, but You are the Lord of all.

Thank you for Your life and Your death. Thank you for Your everlasting love and forgiveness. Thank you for saving us. Thank you for listening to our prayer. In Your holy name, we pray. Amen.

Digging Deeper: What does it mean to you to be able to come before your Savior without fear or trembling? How does this foster a personal relationship with Christ in your faith?

_____

_____

_____

_____

WORDS FOR
EVERYDAY LIVING

You are God! You are almighty and all-powerful, all-knowing, and awesome. Let Your light and Your love shine in our hearts and lives.

You desire to love us, take care of us, and provide for all of our needs. You want what is best for us, and You know positively what is best for our lives.

You are the King of kings and Lord of lords. You have created this world, and You have created each one of us. Help us to live lives worthy of our calling.

We are designed to worship You and praise You with our lives. We need to spend time with You and to love You with our whole hearts and minds and souls, with our entire being.

Thank you for sending Your Son to show us the true way. Thank you for creating us to be Your people and for never leaving us or forsaking us.

Help me to be Your hands and Your feet and to do good in this world for You. Help me to be an ambassador of Your love and to proclaim the good news that You have brought into this world.

When I am selfish and self-centered, I am not seeking to please You. When I am seeking my own wants and desires, I am not looking at others and loving them. When my eyes are focused on me, I can't see the people that You have brought into my life.

Thank you for filling my life with Your blessings and for allowing those blessings to be poured out into the lives of others.

You provide stability and constancy. You are my rock and my fortress. You are my strength and my shield. Help me to keep my eyes focused on You, the author and perfecter of my faith.

Help us to hear Your still, small voice. Help us to distinguish between good and evil. Guide us in the way everlasting. Enable us to hear the voice of our shepherd and to follow the path that leads to You.

Teach us to forgive and to love as You have loved and forgiven us. Forgiveness isn't easy for us.

When we are weak, You are strong. When we are lost, You guide us along the path. When our future looks dark and bleak, You provide the light and hope. You provide for the plants, the vines, and the harvest. You have made the sun to shine, the rain to fall, and the crops to grow.

Your wisdom is greater than ours, and Your thoughts are above ours. You know us better than we know ourselves. The answers You give to us always come in Your perfect timing, not necessarily in our time of crying or sighing.

Through Your life and Your death, You have bridged the gap that sin has created between a Holy Father and His children. You stepped in and carried our burden and our shame. We bow down in humble adoration to You.

Surround us with Your love. Fill us with Your goodness. Strengthen our faith and guide and lead us every step of the way. When we are hopelessly lost, shine Your light into our lives and show us the way.

Help me to be more like You and to desire Your best for me. Help me to be the person that You created me to be. You are mighty and can do all things. Change my heart and draw close to me.

Help us to see people and love people as You do. Help us to look through Your eyes and see our problems as an opportunity to draw closer to You.

We know that in this world there is much evil, but You have overcome this world. You have conquered sin, death, and the devil. In You, we have hope and we have life.

We are imperfect vessels that are cracked and broken. We need to be fixed and to be made whole. We can only be complete when we are in a relationship with You.

Be a light unto our path so that we can lead others to Your light. We want our lives to be a reflection of Your love. We want people to notice the difference in our lives, the difference is You!

We are special to You. You have given us meaning and purpose in life. We come before You reverently filled with awe and wonder. How majestic is Your name, O Lord.

Your world is incredible, and Your creation is amazing. You are awesome, and Your name is greatly to be praised. You are majestic and holy, truly excellent and awe-inspiring.

I know that I am blessed because of You, because of all that You have done for me. In You, I can do all things and be the person that You have created me to be.

You are victorious, and Your name will be praised forever. One day every knee will bow and every tongue will confess that You are Lord! Help us to praise You today with our lives and with our whole hearts.

The wicked will be punished, and those who cling to You will be saved. You provide strength for the weary and hope for the oppressed. You provide abundantly for all Your children, and You know what we need before we even ask!

You have changed our lives forever. You have transformed us from the inside out. You have cleaned out the ugliness, selfishness, and evil within our hearts and replaced them with Your love and kindness.

There is no one that is greater than You. There is no one who is worthy but You. You have conquered all our enemies. You are in control of all things and all people and all nations. You rule the heavens and the earth. You are God.

You long to spend time with us and to be involved in our lives. You are always available with Your arms open wide to comfort us and draw near to us.

You want all people to come to You and lay down their burdens. You want to fill our lives with Your love, joy, and peace. You want to give us hope in this world and for the future.

Before a word is formed and spoken by our mouths, You know it. Before the song rises from our hearts, You hear it. Before the request is made, You know the best possible answer for us.

SECTION 2:

Psalm 11-20

Day 31

In the Lord I take refuge. How then can you say to me: "Flee like a bird to your mountain. For look, the wicked bend their bows; they set their arrows against the strings to shoot from the shadows at the upright in heart. When the foundations are being destroyed, what can the righteous do?"

Psalm 11:1-3

Lord,

You never promised us an easy path. You never promised that our lives would be without problems and concerns. Our lives are on display for all the world to see. Sometimes we are persecuted. Sometimes we face problems. We have tough days. We have pain, and we have sorrow. In this life, nothing will ever be perfect. People aren't perfect; our families and friends may disappoint us; our enemies may take advantage of us; and we may fail in our jobs, at our schools, in our lives. Sometimes our troubles are overwhelming. Sometimes we don't think we can endure. We may want to run away or hide from our fears. It is then that we need to cling to You and hold on to You for dear life. When everything seems to be going wrong, You are always there to carry us through. When we have fallen, You reach out and pick us up. When we are weak, then You are strong. When we are hurting, You are there to comfort us. When it seems like the enemy is winning, we must remember that You are the victor, You have won the battle, You are Almighty and truly amazing.

Thank you for allowing us to seek comfort and refuge in You. Thank you for hearing our prayers. Thank you for providing for all of our needs. We have everything in You. Our rewards may not be in this world, but we will spend all eternity with You. We may not have an easy life, but You have blessed us with the promise of eternal life. Thank you for loving us more than we could know or imagine. Thank you for being our Lord and Savior. Thank you for defeating evil and protecting us from harm.

We humbly come before You in prayer, praising Your name and lifting up our requests to You. Amen.

Digging Deeper: Think of a time when you needed to seek shelter in God's arms. How did God comfort you? What did you learn from this difficult time?

_____

_____

_____

_____

Day 32

The Lord is in his holy temple; the Lord is on his heavenly throne. He observes the sons of men; his eyes examine them. The Lord examines the righteous, but the wicked and those who hate violence his soul hates. For the Lord is righteous, he loves justice; upright men will see his face.

Psalm 11:4-5, 7

Dear Lord,

You are our King. You sit at the right hand of God on Your heavenly throne. You deserve all honor and glory and praise. You have changed the world by leaving Your throne of grace and coming to this world. You were willing to exchange the majesty and beauty of heaven for a humble life as a carpenter. You lived a perfect, spotless, guiltless, blameless, sinless life as our example. You gave of Yourself completely, fulfilling Your mission as our Savior. You emptied Yourself and lovingly died on the cross for us and our sins.

You love all people unconditionally. While we were yet sinners, You died for us! We have done nothing to earn or deserve Your grace. We have been saved through faith alone. We can do nothing to earn eternal life. We are blessed by Your grace and made complete by Your love.

The wicked are lost. They have chosen the ways of this world and not Your ways. They have rejected You and Your love. Yet You continue to show love to all. You long to see Your lost sheep return to You and know You as their shepherd. You have called all people, and You desire to have a relationship with all. Help us to be good witnesses and boldly share our faith and Your love with others. Help us to be a light to the lost and a source of encouragement and strength of the hopeless. We are nothing without You, but in You and through You we can do all things! You are almighty, and nothing is impossible for You.

May Your name be glorified and honored by all people. May You be worshiped and praised. In Your precious name, we pray. Amen.

Digging Deeper: What does it mean that you have been saved through faith alone and that you can't earn your salvation? Why do people think that they can earn their salvation through good works?

_____

_____

_____

_____

Day 33

Help, Lord, for the godly are no more; the faithful have vanished from among men. Everyone lies to his neighbor; their flattering lips speak with deception.

Psalm 12:1-2

Dear Heavenly Father,

You have created this beautiful world and all that is within it. You spoke and the world came into being. Your creative power is displayed throughout the universe. You are an awesome God!

But men have rejected You. They have turned away from You and Your ways. Evil seems to be winning over good. There is so much wickedness in this world. People are seeking their own glory. They are selfish and want everything their own way. People lie and cheat and do anything to get ahead. Your laws and commandments are broken day after day and totally disregarded by the faithless. Deception and lies are commonplace.

But You have overcome evil. Your goodness and love abound in the lives of the faithful. You have not forgotten the godly. You have not overlooked their cries for help. You have crushed Satan and defeated wickedness. You are the way, the truth, and the life. We can come before the Father because You have paved the way. Help us to rely on Your strength to live in this corrupt world. Let Your light shine through our lives. Help us to persevere in this evil world and look forward to an eternity with You.

In Your name we humbly come before You. May Your name forever be praised! Amen.

Digging Deeper: What worldly things or temptations are causing you to stumble in your faith?

_____

_____

_____

_____

Day 34

And the words of the Lord are flawless, like silver refined in a furnace of clay, purified seven times. O Lord, you will keep us safe and protect us from such people forever. The wicked freely strut about when what is vile is honored among men.

Psalm 12:6-8

Dear Lord,

Thank you for giving us Your Word, the Holy Bible. Thank you for teaching us Your will and Your way. Thank you for Your guidance and encouragement. Thank you for providing for our needs through Your Word.

Your Word is flawless. Your Word is perfect. Your Word is precious. It is a treasure for us to read and enjoy. It is a gift from God to be cherished.

"All Scripture is God-breathed and is useful for teaching, rebuking, correcting and training in righteousness" (2 Timothy 3:16). Through Your Word You mold us into the people that You have created us to be. You allow us to go through the fire and experience difficulties so our faith can shine. You burn away the dross and take away the ugliness of our lives so we can brightly shine Your love. As we go through the valley, You have promised to be with us. We need You. We face troubles and trials along life's way, but You have promised to keep us safe and protect us from evil. You are perfect, but we are flawed! Thank you for Your forgiveness and Your everlasting love. Teach us to love others and to cling to You.

Thank you for allowing us to go through difficult times so You can be glorified by our lives. Help us to give of ourselves as You have given to us. Thank you for the many gifts You have given us, especially for Your Word. In the name of Jesus, our Lord and Savior, we pray. Amen.

Digging Deeper: Do you make time on a daily basis to spend with God's precious treasure, His Holy Word? How would more time spent reading the Bible improve your life?

Day 35

How long, O Lord? Will you forget me forever? How long will you hide your face from me? How long must I wrestle with my thoughts and every day have sorrow in my heart? How long will my enemy triumph over me?

Psalm 13:1-2

Dearest Lord and Savior,

How long must we suffer? How long must we wait? Why is everything so difficult? This world is filled with troubles and heartache. People can be cruel. We are beaten down day by day. We are persecuted and under attack. People long to see us fail. They are looking for ways to bring us down. We have many enemies and there is much to fear. We need You, Lord! Please help us to make it through each day. Give us Your unfailing strength and courage. Guide and direct our paths. Make our way clear so we may see You. Shine Your love upon us so we are no longer weary and fearful. Help us to trust in You completely. Help us to always seek Your face. Help us to cling to You and hold on for dear life as the worries of this world become too much for us. We are often distracted from our relationship with You. We are weak and our faith sometimes waivers. We wrestle with doubts and questions. Our minds are filled with worldliness, and our lives are busy with so many things. Help us to focus on You and on our relationship with You. Our enemy, the father of lies, the devil wants to create distance between us and You. He wants to separate us from Your love. He wants to fill our lives with meaningless and empty things. You want what is real and true. You want to bless us and our lives with purpose and meaning. You want to fill our hearts with love and kindness. Satan wants to take our eyes off You and what is most important. He wants to mess up our priorities and keep our lives out of balance.

We need to seek You first, and everything else will fall into place. We need to patiently trust in You and not worry about the things of this world. We need to spend time in prayer so we aren't easily distracted. We need to bring our doubts and fears to You in prayer and seek Your wisdom and guidance. You give us strength for each day and courage along the way.

You have promised to never leave us or forsake us. You would never forget us for You have adopted us into Your family and called us Your own. When we are overwhelmed, calm our hearts. When we are filled with sorrow, comfort us. When we need You, surround us with Your love. We pray all this in Your precious name. Amen.

Digging Deeper: What meaningless and empty things fill your life? What distractions of this world take your eyes off of your relationship with God?

_____

_____

_____

Day 36

Look on me and answer, O Lord my God. Give light to my eyes, or I will sleep in death; my enemy will say, "I have overcome him." And my foes will rejoice when I fall.

Psalm 13:3-4

Dearest Heavenly Father,

Look down on me with love and compassion. When I call out to You, dear Lord, listen to my cries for help. As I pour out my heart to You, I know that You will answer me. Watch over me like a shepherd who watches over his sheep and protects them with his life. Guard me from evil and from the evil one who wants to drag me away from You forever. Do not let my enemies or the pressures of this world overcome me. I know that You have triumphed over all things, You are above all things. You are almighty and all-powerful. You can do anything and everything. Shine Your light over me so that no one will attack me in the night. Do not let darkness and the prince of darkness lead me astray. Protect me from all harm. Keep me safe in Your loving arms. Draw near to me so that nothing will happen to me. I trust in You completely. You are my Savior and my God. My life is in Your hands. When I fall, pick me up and carry me. When I fail, remind me that I am Your child and I am forgiven. When I hurt someone, help me to seek forgiveness from them and from You. When I am lost, gently guide me back into Your arms.

Although my enemy wants to destroy me, help me to love him as You love him. Even though my foes want to lead me into the traps of this world, help me to keep my eyes firmly focused on You. Be my comfort and guide in the craziness of this world. Be my Father and show me Your perfect way! I pray all these things in the name, of Jesus, my Lord and Savior, the Good Shepherd who has poured out his life for me. Amen.

Digging Deeper: What are some practical ways that you can love your enemies? How can you live your faith "out loud" so it is visible to others?

_____

_____

_____

_____

Day 37

But I trust in your unfailing love; my heart rejoices in your salvation. I will sing to the Lord, for he has been good to me.

Psalm 13:5-6

Dear Lord,

Your love for us is amazing and incomprehensible. Your Word says that You have loved us with an "everlasting love." Your love is unconditional. There is nothing we can do to earn or deserve Your love. You are love! In You alone is our love complete. We have love because You first loved us and You have taught us how to love.

Help us to show Your love to others and shine Your light to our family and friends. We pray that Your love would work in our hearts and lives to mold us and shape us into the people You have created us to be. Create in us a new heart and replace the evil in our lives with Your good. Let us praise You with our lips, our words, our songs, and our lives. We need You and Your incredible love. We rejoice in the many blessings we have received from You. We give You all thanks and praise for Your generosity and Your loving-kindness. You are so good to us! We are not always good to You or to the people that You have brought into our lives. Thank you for Your precious gift of forgiveness. Thank you for accepting us for who we are. We know that we are not perfect, only You are perfect! We know that we fail time after time, only You are victorious in every situation. We are sinful and You alone are without sin.

Draw near to us as we worship You. Bless us as we read Your Word and spend time with You in prayer. Be our guide and show us Your will for our lives. Thank you for Your life and the example You are. Help us to be more like You. In Your holy name, we pray. Amen.

Digging Deeper: How do you explain God's unconditional love to someone? How has God's love changed your life?

Day 38

The fool says in his heart, "There is no God." They are corrupt, their deeds are vile; there is no one who does good. The Lord looks down from heaven on the sons of men to see if there are any who understand, any who seek God.

Psalm 14:1-2

Dear Father,

You have blessed us with every spiritual gift and given us Your love in abundance. When we ask, You give us wisdom and strength. You have given us courage to face every challenge that comes before us. You know what we need before we even ask.

The wise man seeks You, but the foolish man rejects You. The wise man fears and loves the Lord. The foolish man fears no one. The wise man seeks to know God. The foolish man says there is no God. Without Your guidance and love, people in this world are lost and without hope. You long to spend time with us, Your children. As a father in this world longs to love and care for his child, so much more do You, our Heavenly Father, want to have a relationship with us. You desire to give us every blessing and watch over us. You wait for us with open arms. You surround us with Your unconditional love. Your ability to give and to forgive is unsurpassed. It's an amazing love!

The foolish man rejects You, Your love, Your will, Your ways, and Your Word. He loses out in this life and for all eternity. He is corrupt, evil, sinful, and vile. But we are all wicked. The desires of our heart are selfish and corrupt. It is only by Your grace that we are saved. Dear Father, only You are good, only You are loving, only You are perfect! Teach us to be wise and not foolish! Thank you for calling us Your children and for Your life-changing love. Thank you for being our Father.

We humbly come before You in the name of Jesus, Your Son, our Lord and Savior. Amen.

Digging Deeper: Do you encounter foolish people in your daily life? How do these foolish people affect your efforts to live a faithful live? How does God help us to avoid the pitfalls that entrap foolish people?

Day 39

All have turned aside, they have together become corrupt; there is no one who does good, not even one. Will evildoers never learn—those who devour my people as men eat bread and who do not call on the Lord? There they are, overwhelmed with dread, for God is present in the company of the righteous.

Psalm 14:3-5

Dear Heavenly Father,

Your people have turned away from You. They are corrupt and evil. There is no good in them. They seek to devour others and lead them astray. People are only concerned with themselves and their well-being. They are looking out for number one.

Help us to focus our eyes on You and allow You to be number one in our hearts and lives. Help us to call upon Your name and seek to do Your will. As people seek to work harder and earn more money and gain more things, they never seem to be satisfied. We have a void in our lives, an emptiness inside. We try to fill it with all kinds of things. We desire attention, power, money, glory, fame, popularity, and happiness. In this world, these desires may be filled temporarily, but the feelings don't last. We want more. We need more. It doesn't matter what we do or who we hurt in the process. Only in You can we experience real peace and joy. Only You can fill the emptiness in our souls. Only You know what is best for us.

Help us to love people as You love them. Enable us to love our neighbors as ourselves. We want to be Christ-centered and not self-centered. We should build people up instead of tear them apart. We should shine Your light and love instead of seeking to fulfill our own needs and desires. We are selfish by nature. Show us how to be more like You!

We ask this in Jesus' name, our Lord and Savior, the author and perfecter of our faith. Amen.

Digging Deeper: What kinds of things have you tried to fill the God-shaped void in your life? How has that worked for you? What would work better?

_____

_____

_____

_____

Day 40

You evildoers frustrate the plans of the poor, but the Lord is their refuge. Oh, that salvation for Israel would come out of Zion! When the Lord restores the fortunes of his people, let Jacob rejoice and Israel be glad!

Psalm 14:6-7

Dear Heavenly Father,

You are the God of Abraham, Isaac, and Jacob. You have chosen Israel and created a covenant with them. You are their God, and they are Your people. You led them out of bondage in Egypt. You traveled with them in the desert for forty years and provided for all their needs. You led them to the "promised land," the land of milk and honey. You delivered them from their enemies and gave the land to Your people.

You want all people to come to know You. You have called the Jews and the Gentiles to be Your children. You want to have a relationship with all people. As You led Israel to the promised land long ago, so You will lead us to our eternal home in heaven.

Your message was delivered to the Jews and also to the Gentiles. Jesus went to the synagogues and the temple, and his disciples were called to share Your Word and Your love to the four corners of the earth. You desire to see all people saved. You have called each of us to be Your witnesses. We should love You with our whole heart and soul and mind. Our lives should reflect You. We are called to give an answer for the hope that we have. Give us boldness and courage to reach out in faith and share our hearts. Give us the words to say and help us to take advantage of the opportunities that we are given. Help us to be a light to all people so both Jews and Gentiles can rejoice with You forever!

We ask that Your Spirit would guide us along the way. We pray this in Jesus' name. Amen.

Digging Deeper: How do you feel about being called to be God's witness? Why are you afraid to share your faith? What words of God give you comfort and hope to share with others?

_____

_____

_____

_____

Day 41

Lord, who may dwell in your sanctuary? Who may live on your holy hill? He whose walk is blameless and who does what is righteous, who speaks the truth from his heart and has no slander on his tongue, who does his neighbor no wrong and casts no slur on his fellow man.

Psalm 15:1-3

Dearest Lord,

No one is able to come before You. No one is worthy. We are all sinners. We are not righteous or perfect. We are not blameless or pure. Our hearts are filled with evil and our words aren't filled with praise. We don't build each other up, we tear each other down. We don't seek to please God, we indulge our selfish nature. We don't speak the truth in love as Your Word teaches us, sometimes our words are hurtful and angry instead of encouraging and loving.

Lord, You are perfect and we can't live up to Your standards. We fail, we fall short, and we are evil and sometimes heartless. We step on others to boost ourselves. We tear people down so we feel better about ourselves. Teach us to be loving and positive instead of hateful and negative. Show us how to sing Your praises and glorify You with our words, our thoughts, our actions, and our lives. We should use our words for praises and not curses. We need to be more like You. Take away the evil in our lives. Examine our hearts and show us where we need to grow. We can do all things through You and

Your strength. We humbly come before You, unworthy of Your love. Forgive us our sins and show us Your will for our lives.

We ask this in the name of our holy and blameless Lord and Savior. Amen.

Digging Deeper: Examine the words that come out of your mouth. Do they edify or destroy others? Are your words positive or negative? How can you do a better job of praising God and loving others through your words?

_____

_____

_____

_____

Day 42

Who despises a vile man but honors those who fear the Lord, who keeps his oath even when it hurts, who lends his money without usury and does not accept a bribe against the innocent. He who does these things will never be shaken.

Psalm 15:4-5

Oh Dearest Lord,

You are worthy of honor and praise, glory and adoration. We are to fear and love You. We should respect You and live our lives in a manner that is pleasing to You. You have given us Your holy Word, the Bible, to teach us how to live. You showed us how to live by Your perfect example. It is impossible for us to live a perfect life, but nothing is impossible for You.

We struggle in this life. We make poor decisions. We don't do what we should do. We do the things that we shouldn't. We fall short of Your standard of perfection, but You are always there to pick us up and rescue us. You forgive us. You love us unconditionally. Teach us how to live and how to love. Help us to honor You with our lives. Help us to keep our oaths and live by our word. Help us to be trustworthy and honorable. Be our Rock and our fortress. When our lives are shaken and we begin to doubt, be our strength and guide. Sustain our faith and guard our hearts. Gently remind us that we are never alone. You have promised to be with us always. In this world, we will have trouble, we will be tempted, and we will have trials and difficult times. Thank you for never giving up on us.

May Your name be praised now and forevermore! We lift up our requests to You and ask all these things in Your precious name. Amen.

Digging Deeper: Review your decision-making process. How do you recover from poor decisions? How can you use God's tools to help you make better decisions?

_____

_____

_____

_____

Day 43

Keep me safe, O God, for in you I take refuge. I said to the Lord, "You are my Lord; apart from you I have no good thing."

Psalm 16:1-2

Dear Heavenly Father,

You love us as Your precious children. You have created us and You know us. We know that we can trust You with our lives. You are committed to us and devoted to us. In You, we have life. In You, we are safe. You are our refuge and our strength. You promised to be with us always, to never leave us or forsake us. When times are tough, You are there. When things are going well, You are there. When we feel lost and alone, You are there. When the world seems to be crashing down on top of us, You are there. When we are hurting, You are there. When we are mourning the loss of someone special, You are there. When we are in need, You are there.

You love us more than we even love ourselves. You care about every aspect of our lives. You know our thoughts, our dreams, our goals, our desires, and our hearts. You are listening to our prayers and watching over us. In You, we are complete. In Your Son's blood, we are made clean. When we are wrapped in Your love, You see us as perfect. The only "good" in us comes from You. Without You, we are nothing.

We need You each and every day. We need Your love and forgiveness, Your guidance and leadership. Shine through us so the world may see You and Your goodness in our lives. We lift up these requests in the name of our Lord and Savior, Jesus Christ. Amen.

Digging Deeper: In what ways does God's goodness shine through you? What gifts, talents and blessings has God given to you? How can you use them for His glory?

_____

_____

_____

_____

Day 44

I will praise the Lord, who counsels me; even at night my heart instructs me. I have set the Lord always before me. Because he is at my right hand, I will not be shaken.

Psalm 16:7-8

Dear Lord,

I will praise You today and every day. I will lift up Your holy name. You left the splendors and majesty of heaven to come to earth. You came to be my Savior and to show me the one true way. You came to lead me to the Father and restore my relationship with Him. You came to give me life and teach me the truth. You have given me Your Spirit to uplift and encourage me, counsel and guide me. Your Holy Spirit gently reminds me of You and Your Word. You have promised to always be with me. You love me with an everlasting love. Because of You, I will not fear. I will not be afraid because You are always by my side. You will never leave me. I am Yours forever. I may stumble and fall, but You will reach out Your hand and pick me up. Although I may have doubts, my faith will not be shaken.

Lord, teach me to trust in You and in Your Word. Allow Your Spirit to soften my heart, and make me more like You. Continue to instruct me and counsel me that I may always walk with You. Help me to keep my eyes focused on Your will for my life and Your best for me. You created me, and You know me better than I know myself. You have blessed me abundantly. I need You in my life. You are my Lord and Savior, the solid rock upon which I have built my faith. You are the cornerstone upon which I have built my life. You provide me with a firm foundation. Thank you for Your love and for Your forgiveness. Thank you for sending Your Spirit to speak to my heart and instruct me each day. Thank you for saving me. In Your holy name, I pray. Amen.

Digging Deeper: How does the Holy Spirit work in your life? How does God's Spirit comfort and encourage you?

_____

_____

_____

_____

Day 45

Therefore my heart is glad and my tongue rejoices; my body also will rest secure, because you will not abandon me to the grave, nor will you let your Holy One see decay. You have made known to me the path of life; you will fill me with joy in your presence, with eternal pleasures at your right hand.

Psalm 16:9-11

Dear Heavenly Father,

You have filled my heart with gladness. You have given me true hope! You provide guidance along the path of life. In You, I have life and love. You fill me with joy! Thank you for allowing me to come into Your presence. I rejoice in You and praise Your holy name.

There are times when I don't know what I should do; times when I am lost and I feel alone. There are days when I feel ineffective and unimportant. There are moments when I feel like life is so chaotic and I have no control. Sometimes, I hurt and I don't know where to turn. Life is busy and there are many pressures, troubles, trials, and temptations that each person faces. Father, I know that You love me. I know that You care about every aspect of my life. You want to comfort me when my heart is breaking. You send Your Spirit to show me the way. You sent Your Son to be a perfect example and to teach us about Your Love. You are in control and You can do all things. I need to trust in You and not rely on myself. I need a Father to take care of me. I need Jesus to be my Savior, and I need the guidance, comfort, and encouragement of Your Holy Spirit. You have given me all things! Let me praise Your name and share Your love with those around me. Continue to work in me and create in me a new heart, one that better reflects Your love and light. Forgive me of my sins and teach me Your will for my life.

I love You. Thank you for being my Father and allowing me to be Your child. I pray all these things and lift up the requests on my heart in the name of Your Son, Jesus. Amen.

Digging Deeper: What does the Psalmist mean by "You will fill me with joy in Your presence"? Have you ever experienced this type of joy?

_____

_____

_____

_____

Day 46

Hear, O Lord, my righteous plea; listen to my cry. Give ear to my prayer—it does not rise from deceitful lips. May my vindication come from you; may your eyes see what is right.

Psalm 17:1-2

Dear Lord,

Sometimes our prayers are quiet whispers. Sometimes our prayers are cries for help. Sometimes our prayers are groans from the deepest parts of our hearts. Sometimes we cry out pleading for help and guidance. Sometimes the pains are so deep that we can't find the words to say and we just need to dwell in Your presence and seek comfort from You.

Lord, you know our hearts. You know the words we are going to say before they are on our tongues. Help us to speak the truth in love and not to be deceitful. Give us the words to say as we share our hearts and our faith. May we always do what is right and seek to follow your perfect path. Remove the sin and guilt and all the things that make us ineffective witnesses for you. Take away everything that hinders our relationship with You. Bless our time of worship and prayer. Provide for our needs so we can take care of the needs of those around us. Teach us to rely on You completely for our every need. Listen to our quiet whispers and our cries for help, and answer each prayer with Your perfect wisdom and timing. In Jesus' name we pray. Amen.

Digging Deeper: Do you rely on God as much as you should? How can you put all of your life into his hands?

_____

_____

_____

_____

Day 47

Though you probe my heart and examine me at night, though you test me, you will find nothing; I have resolved that my mouth will not sin. As for the deeds of men—by the word of my lips I have kept myself from the ways of the violent.

Psalm 17:3-4

Dear Lord,

Lead us not into temptation and deliver us from evil. Help us to flee from the temptations of the devil. He wants to devour us. He wants to destroy us. He is the father of lies. He is clever, and he knows our weaknesses. Help us to stay away from the places that we are tempted. Help us to avoid people who are not good influences for us. Keep us safe in Your loving arms. Help us to do the good that You have created us to do and not the evil that is all around us.

No matter how hard we try, we are not good. We sin, we make mistakes, we hurt people, and we even disappoint You. We want to be the people that You have created us to be. We want to be a shining light and a good example to others in this world. We aren't perfect, and we will never be perfect. Shine Your light into our hearts, and show us where we fall short. Create a clean heart within us. Remove the evil from our lips, our thoughts, our minds, and our souls. Help us to love You with our whole heart and to clean out the areas of ugliness and evil within our souls. We pray that You would send Your Spirit to convict us and show us our sins. We ask for Your forgiveness that You have given to us through Your Son, Jesus Christ. He came so we might have life and know the way, the truth, and the life. He came to lead us to You. We love You and ask for Your forgiveness. Give us boldness and courage to live out our faith every day of our lives.

We ask this in the name of Jesus, our Savior and Lord. Amen.

Digging Deeper: What are your weaknesses? What things tempt you? How can you avoid these temptations?

_____

_____

_____

_____

Day 48

I call on you, O God, for you will answer me; give ear to me and hear my prayer. Show the wonder of your great love, you who save by your right hand those who take refuge in you from their foes.

Psalm 17:6-7

Dear God,

You are my beloved Heavenly Father. You love me like no earthly father could. Your love is real and complete. Your love fills my heart and my life and gives me a sense of purpose and meaning. You are everything to me. You have created me and given me life in this place and time. You are always with me to listen to me, love me, forgive me, sustain me, encourage me, and take care of my every need. I deserve nothing, yet You have given me everything. I lack nothing that is needed. You have listened to my prayers and answered them in the best way possible. My trust is in You alone. You have loved me with an everlasting love, one that is too great to even believe.

You have blessed me with Your Holy Spirit to guide me in this world. You have sent Your Son to be my Savior and Lord. You have created this beautiful world for me to dwell. Your majesty and Your awesome power are displayed throughout the universe. And yet, You take time to hear my prayer. You reveal Yourself to me in all things. Wherever I look, You can be found. Wherever I seek, I will find You and Your great love. You do not condemn me for my sins. You shower me with forgiveness. You protect me from harm, and the evil that is all around me. I need You today and every day. Help me to cling to You and Your Word. Guard my heart and fill it completely with Your love. In the name of Jesus, Your Son, I humbly come before You in prayer. Amen.

Digging Deeper: How do you interact with each part of the Holy Trinity: the Father, Son and Holy Spirit?

_____

_____

_____

_____

Day 49

Keep me as the apple of your eye; hide me in the shadow of your wings from the wicked who assail me, from my mortal enemies who surround me. They close up their callous hearts, and their mouths speak with arrogance.

Psalm 17:9-10

Dear God,

Thank you for loving me and for choosing me to be Your child. Thank you for holding me in the palm of Your righteous hand and keeping me safe from the evil all around me. Thank you for protecting me from the wicked and keeping my enemies away from me. They long to see me broken and hurting. They want to succeed at all costs, and they tear apart any and all who are in their way. Your way is perfect. Your way is right. Your way is filled with love. Their ways are treacherous and dangerous. They want to destroy others to get ahead in this world. They seek glory and power for themselves. They are filled with arrogance and pride. They are greedy, wanting what they cannot have and seeking to obtain all things at any cost.

You deserve the glory and honor. You are the King of kings. You alone are worthy of praise. Your way is not easy, but You have promised to be with me on every step of the path. When times are hard, You will give me courage to press on. I want to honor You with my life and with my work. I want Your will to be done on earth and in heaven. You are almighty, and You are in control of all things. One day the wicked will be punished. Those who have hardened their hearts and turned against You will be judged. Those who love You will be led along the everlasting path and spend eternity praising You. Help me always to trust in Your loving-kindness and Your perfect way. In the name of Jesus, Your Son and my Lord and Savior, I pray. Amen.

Digging Deeper: Why should the wicked be punished? Who are your enemies, and what impact do they have on your life?

_____

_____

_____

_____

Day 50

Rise up, O Lord, confront them, bring them down; rescue me from the wicked by your sword. O Lord, by your hand save me from such men, from men of this world whose reward is in this life.

Psalm 17:13-14a

Dear Lord,

The ways of this world are corrupt and evil. It seems like the wicked prevail. The righteous suffer, and those who seek to fulfill their own desires prosper. You are holy and just. You will punish the wicked in Your time. Although some people may gain the whole world if they have lost their souls they will have nothing. The riches, wealth, fame, and power of this world are temporary. Only with You as our Lord and Savior will we have eternal life. This world is passing away and will be gone in an instant. We will either have eternity to spend worshiping and praising You, or we will be separated from You and Your love forever. We can store up for ourselves treasures in heaven, those with eternal value or we can try to gather treasures for this world only.

You have given us every blessing. You have given us every good gift. We know that all we have comes from You. Take away our pride and allow us to humbly come before You in prayer. Take away our evil desires and help us to desire to do Your will. Take away our greed and help us seek eternal rewards. Open our eyes so we can see the world as You do. Open our hearts to love others as You love them. Open our minds to accept Your wisdom and Your ways. Help us to resist the evil one and his lies and to seek You and Your truths. Rescue us from ourselves and the evil within us. Draw us nearer to You and help us to hear Your still, quiet voice amidst the chaos of this world. You are God, and You can do all things. Renew our hearts and strengthen our faith. Give us an eternal perspective. We ask all these things in Your precious name, dear Lord and Savior. Amen.

Digging Deeper: What is an eternal perspective? How do you determine your priorities? What is most important to you?

_____

_____

_____

_____

Day 51

I love you, O Lord, my strength. The Lord is my rock, my fortress and my deliverer; my God is my rock, in whom I take refuge. He is my shield and the horn of my salvation, my stronghold.

Psalm 18:1-2

Dear Lord, my God,

I love You today and every day, always and forever. You give my life meaning. You provide for my needs. You listen to my prayers. You are my strength and my deliverer. You watch over me. You care about every aspect of my life. You love me!

The ways of this world are evil. There are so many things that drag us down. The problems of this world take our eyes off You. The news is depressing. People are suffering, people are dying, and many people are hurting. There are problems, troubles, and trials everywhere you look. When we try to handle things ourselves, everything gets worse! We need You! You are our rock! You are unchangeable, a solid foundation on which we can build our faith. You are our refuge! You are our hiding place. We need the solace and the peace that You provide. We are broken, we are beaten, and we are discouraged. You are our salvation. You are our redeemer. When we are bogged down and overwhelmed by this world, You are always there waiting to guide and lead us through each day. When we are stressed, we can come to You for comfort and peace. We need Your strength. We need Your love and encouragement. We need the peace that only You can provide. We can't make it on our own. We need a Savior!

Thank you for doing what we are unable to do. Thank you for Your support and encouragement. Thank you for Your everlasting love. We praise Your name and lift up our requests to You. Amen.

Digging Deeper: How do you describe peace? When do you feel peaceful? Have you experienced God's "peace that passes all understanding"?

Day 52

I call to the Lord who is worthy of praise, and I am saved from my enemies. In my distress I called to the Lord; I cried to my God for help. From his temple he heard my voice; my cry came before him, into his ears.

Psalm 18:3, 6

Dear Lord,

You alone are worthy of our praise, our attention, our focus, and our adoration. You have given Your love to us and even given us Your life. You are the perfect example for us. You have demonstrated to us how we should live our lives. You have overcome evil. You have triumphed over sin. You have defeated our enemies. In our distress, You come to us. You are always there whenever we call.

Thank you for listening to our prayers. Thank you for hearing our cries of distress and our pleas for help. Thank you for taking care of us and answering our prayers in the best possible way. You have been merciful and kind to us. You have protected us from our enemies, and You will always be available to us when we need Your help. You have saved us from trouble, sheltered us from the storms of life, and carried us through difficult days and times. Nothing is too hard for You. Nothing is impossible. You are the Almighty God. We need You because on our own, we get lost. We wander off and lose our way. We get caught up in the glitter and excitement of this world, and we lose our focus. We need to trust in You completely.

We need to pour out our hearts to You and draw near to You. We cannot make it on our own. You are our Savior and our Lord. You are worthy of our devotion and our love. We praise Your holy name. We bow down before You. As You reign from Your throne above, we ask You to reign in our hearts. We want You to be on the throne of our lives. Help us to seek You first and to desire to do Your will for our lives. Teach us to love and forgive unconditionally. We yield control of our lives to You knowing that You are the potter and we are the clay. Make something beautiful out of our lives. We ask all these things in the name of Jesus, our Lord. Amen.

Digging Deeper: How does God work to make something beautiful in your life on a daily basis?

_____

_____

_____

_____

Day 53

He rescued me from my powerful enemy, from my foes, who were too strong for me. They confronted me in the day of my disaster, but the Lord was my support. He brought me out into a spacious place; he rescued me because he delighted in me.

Psalm 18:17-19

Dearest Lord and Savior,

Day after day, You rescue me. You provide the strength and courage that I need each day. Life in this world can be difficult. Some problems are hard to face alone. Thank you for being with me at all times and providing for my needs every day. Thank you for pulling me out of the pit of my troubles and trials and walking with me on solid ground. Thank you for being the rock of my salvation and the cornerstone of my faith. You are my support. You are my comforter. You are my Savior. Although my enemy is powerful and very real, You have defeated all my enemies and You are almighty. Although the ways of this world are enticing and distracting, You have overcome all temptation and are the perfect example for us. Although I am sinful, I make mistakes, and I fall short in many ways, You still love me. You delight in me. You accept me, and I am part of Your family. There is no greater love than this!

Teach me how to love unconditionally. Teach me to be patient with those who make mistakes and who hurt me. Teach me how to forgive others as You have forgiven me.

Help me not to be judgmental and condemning. Show me Your will for my life and help me to be a good ambassador for Your kingdom. Let Your kindness and love flow through my life and touch the lives of others. Fill me with Your goodness and take away the sinfulness and evil that are in my life. Cleanse me and renew my heart. Send Your Holy Spirit to guide me and encourage me. Give me strength to face my enemies and be strong in my faith. Forgive me all my sins! Thank you for the abundant blessings we have in You. In Your precious name, I pour out my heart and lift up these requests. Amen.

Digging Deeper: It is so easy for us to judge others. How can we learn to be more forgiving and loving to other people?

_____

_____

_____

_____

Day 54

To the faithful you show yourself to be faithful, to the blameless you show yourself blameless, to the pure You show yourself pure, but to the crooked you show yourself shrewd. You save the humble but bring low those whose eyes are haughty.

Psalm 18:25-27

Dear Lord,

You are all things to all people, but You are always true to Your character and faithful to Your Father. You are perfect. You are holy. You are strong. You are everlasting. You are the Alpha and the Omega, the beginning and the end. You are now and always will be the foundation of our faith and the stronghold of our lives. You are faithful, and You have been faithful unto death. You followed Your Father's plan and completed His work on earth. You were the lamb that was slain for us. You are the plan of salvation. You are perfect and blameless, holy and pure, a living sacrifice. You came to this world to be all that we could not be and to do all that we could not do. You lived a life without sin but we are sinful every day. You spent time with Your Father in prayer seeking His will for Your life. We try to do things on our own using our wisdom and strength, but we fail and fall short. You have never failed. You have never fallen short. You came to be an example for us and to show us the way. You are the truth and Your life is filled with the truth and love that only come from the Father. Because of Your life, we have been given eternal life. You have paid the price for our sins. Through You, we can come before the Father. In You, we are seen as perfect. The penalty of our sin has been paid by Your blood. We are not worthy of Your grace, but it has freely been given to us. You have given our lives purpose and meaning. You have restored our relationship with our heavenly Father. You are the way, the truth, and the life, and no one can come to the Father except through You. Thank you for being our Savior. Thank you for being faithful, even unto death. Thank you for the gift of faith and everlasting life. Thank you for loving us today, tomorrow, and always. We give You thanks and praise for You alone are worthy. In Your holy name, we humbly come before our Father in prayer. Amen.

Digging Deeper: What descriptive words do you use to describe the character of God? What qualities do you long to possess?

Day 55

You, O Lord, keep my lamp burning; my God turns my darkness into light. With your help I can advance against a troop, with my God I can scale a wall. As for God, his way is perfect; the word of the Lord is flawless. He is a shield for all who take refuge in him.

Psalm 18:28-30

Dear God, our Father,

Thank you for all that You do for us. You are our sunshine, and You cause the sun to rise every morning. You have filled the night skies with the moon and the stars. You turn darkness into light, and You light the path of our lives. You provide strength and courage for each new day. In You and through You, we can do all things. Nothing is impossible for You. You are our almighty God, the Creator of the world and the lover of our souls. You help us along the way and guide our every step. You keep us safe. You love us with an everlasting love. You are perfect, and Your plan for our lives is the absolute best for us. We should desire to do Your will, but we are often distracted. We don't seek You and Your infinite wisdom first. We unsuccessfully try to do things our way. We want to be in control of everything. We want to live our lives our way. But we need You! You are our strength and our shield. Your love fills our lives and touches the lives of those around us. When we are self-serving, we are ineffective. When we are using our own power, we are weak.

When we are fulfilling our desires, we are lost. When we do things on our own, we often fail miserably.

We need You, dear Father! We need to be in Your Word, listening to Your wisdom, learning Your ways. Although we are often weak and shortsighted, You are always strong and Your ways are eternal. We lose our focus and our way, but You are willing and anxious to hold our hand and let us follow in Your footsteps. You never fail us or desert us. You have promised to never leave us. You forgive us every day when we fail, when we mess up, when we fall short. Your grace is sufficient to meet all our needs, and Your love is amazing and never-ending. You are our perfect and holy Heavenly father. Thank you for filling our lives with love, kindness, and forgiveness when we deserve Your anger, punishment, and wrath. We deserve so little, yet You have blessed us with so much! Great is Your faithfulness! Teach us to be faithful and loving to You and others. In the name of Your Son, our Lord, we pray. Amen.

Digging Deeper: When has the world seemed like a dark and lonely place to you? What are some ways that God has brought light into your life and onto your path?

Day 56

For who is God besides the Lord? And who is the Rock except our God? It is God who arms me with strength and makes my way perfect. You give me your shield of victory, and your right hand sustains me.

Psalm 18:31, 35a

Dear God,

Forgive us when we try to run our own lives and do things our way. Forgive us when we try to control every aspect of our lives and sometimes the lives of others. Forgive us when we seek to fulfill our own wants and desires. Forgive us when we make selfish decisions. Forgive us when we hurt those around us. Forgive us when we don't do what we should do. Forgive us when we do the things we shouldn't do. We are sinful. We are self-centered. Our hearts are evil. We often fail and fall short of Your perfect standard. Sometimes we think that we know everything. We believe that our way is best, and we want things our way.

You alone are God. You alone are perfect. You alone are holy. There is no one like You! Your love is unconditional. Your ways are flawless. Your thoughts are so far above our thoughts. Your Word is powerful. Your power is without limits. Your strength is beyond anything we can imagine. You have created us and You can sustain us. You know us completely, and yet You still love us. You see our shortcomings and our imperfections. You know our evil desires and our unloving thoughts. You see into our hearts.

Purify our hearts and minds. Show us Your perfect ways and help us to live our lives in a manner that is pleasing to You. Take away our imperfections and the evil in our lives. Forgive us our sins. Show us the way, the truth, and the life. Reveal Yourself in our lives and help us to share Your goodness and love with others. Help us to cling to You and fill our lives with Your perfect love. Continue to work in our lives. Thank you for never giving up on us! You alone are God! Thank you for working in our lives! We pray for strength and courage to face each new day with You. Thank you for Your abundant blessings. In Jesus' name we pray. Amen.

Digging Deeper: How does God use the people around you to show His perfect ways? Who are the people around you who fortify your spiritual relationship with God?

_____

_____

_____

_____

Day 57

The heavens declare the glory of God; the skies proclaim the work of his hands. Day after day they pour forth speech; night after night they display knowledge. There is no speech or language where their voice is not heard. Their voice goes out into all the earth, their words to the ends of the world.

Psalm 19:1-4a

Dear Heavenly Father,

You are the Creator of the universe. You have carefully and wonderfully made each one of us. You have set the entire world into motion. The moon and the stars reflect light in the night sky, and the sun shines radiantly during the daytime hours. Throughout creation the amazing work of Your hands is displayed. The beauty and wonder and awe of Your power is visible to all. The universe is filled with Your glory and majesty! All nations and all people in this world can look around and see evidence of Your work. The heavens declare Your glory! Throughout the world, evidence of Your creative power is displayed.

As we watch the sunset and the glorious colors filling the sky, we are amazed. As the waves crash to the shore, we are awed. As the stars twinkle in the sky, our attention is captured and drawn to our Creator. You alone are God. You have created all things. You are awe inspiring! Your work is captivating!

Thank you for creating us and for guiding and directing our paths. As You have put the world into motion, so You carefully and wonderfully watch over the details of our lives. You are our Father. You love us completely. Thank you for listening to our prayers as we humbly come before You. There is no one who is like You. No one can compare to You. Your majesty and power are displayed throughout the universe, and You have changed my heart! Thank you for Your life-changing love! Thank you for who You are and for what You are doing in this world and in my life. You are all powerful! We humbly come before You. You alone are worthy of our praise, "To God be the glory forever and ever!" In the name of Jesus, we humbly pray. Amen.

Digging Deeper: What parts of God's creation most inspire you? Where do you feel close to God?

_____

_____

_____

_____

Day 58

The law of the Lord is perfect, reviving the soul. The statutes of the Lord are trustworthy, making wise the simple. The precepts of the Lord are right, giving joy to the heart. The commands of the Lord are radiant, giving light to the eyes. The fear of the Lord is pure, enduring forever.

Psalm 19:7-9a

Dear Lord,

We need help. We need direction. We need guidance. We need You. You are wise beyond belief. You are perfect in every way. You are holy and just. You know all things. You are our Creator and our Redeemer. You came to this world to show us how to live. Thank you for giving us Your Word to instruct us in Your ways. Thank you for giving us Your truth to guide us in this complex world. Thank you for giving us guidelines to live our lives and commands to follow. We trust in You completely. You have given us Your laws to protect us, to keep us from harm, and to draw us closer to You. As a parent longs to love and protect their children, so You long to watch over us and guide us along the way. You have lovingly given us Your commands for our own benefit. Your discipline helps us grow in our faith and helps to build our character. Your instruction helps us learn. Your love is revealed to us in Your Word. You want what is best for us. You don't want to see us ruin our lives by hurting ourselves and others. As we seek to do Your will and follow Your ways, our lives are filled with joy and contentment. We are not merely seeking what is best for us, we are seeking Your best for us. Your statutes are trustworthy, Your precepts are right, and Your laws are perfect. You have given us Your best. You have given us Your life. All we have comes from You.

Help us to cling to You and to hold on to You and Your Word. You are our rock. You are our Savior. You provide strength, hope, and courage for each new day. When we fail, You are always there to help us. When we fall, You encourage us to start again. When we are weak, You are our strength. When we sin, You forgive us. Even though we are imperfect, You still love us. Thank you for Your never-ending patience and Your loving-kindness. You are perfect! Help us to learn from the Master and the greatest teacher, our Savior and Lord. Amen.

Digging Deeper: How does God's law revive the soul? What role do God's commands play in your life?

Day 59

The ordinances of the Lord are sure and altogether righteous. They are more precious than gold, than much pure gold; they are sweeter than honey, than honey from the comb. May the words of my mouth and the meditation of my heart be pleasing in your sight, O Lord, my Rock and my Redeemer.

Psalm 19:9a-10, 14

Dear Lord,

Sometimes we come before You and pour out our hearts. We aren't always sure what to say or how to say it. Sometimes we bow before You and weep because we are sinful and unworthy. Sometimes we are quiet and still as we seek Your presence and Your comfort. Sometimes our prayers are jumbled and confused because we do not know how to pray. Sometimes our prayers are songs of worship, praises to our Lord, words and songs from our heart. Sometimes our prayers are tears of sorrow, anguish, pain, hurting, and suffering. You have promised to listen to us and to answer our prayers. You can always make sense of our babbling even when we don't know what we are trying to say. You understand our confusion. Sometimes You speak to us in a still, small voice. Sometimes we are touched by the beauty of Your creation and the colors of Your world. Sometimes we are awed by Your majesty.

Sometimes it seems that we are too busy to pray. We keep going at a crazy pace until our day is interrupted or our world changes, and we need to stop and take note. We want to be in control. We want to do things on our own. We are selfish and self-centered. We need to look at things and at people as You do, not as the world does. We need to follow Your instruction and Your guidance and seek You, not desire things. In the midst of chaos, You provide peace. When we are uncertain of our future, we can trust You because You know the way. When we are tempted, You provide a way out. When we are hurting, You are there to comfort us. We are flawed, but You are perfect in every way.

Thank you for listening to our prayers, our words, our cries, and our pleas. Thank you for answering us in the best possible way. "May the words of my mouth and the meditation of my heart be pleasing in Your sight, O Lord, my rock and my redeemer." In Your precious name, we humbly come before You. Amen.

Digging Deeper: Are the words of your mouth and the meditation of your heart pleasing to God? In what ways can you grow and improve in this area of your life?

Julie Walker Mitchell

Day 60

May the Lord answer you when you are in distress; may the name of the God of Jacob protect you. May he send you help from the sanctuary and grant you support from Zion. May he give you the desire of your heart and make all your plans succeed.

Psalm 20:1-2, 4

Dear Lord,

Your name is holy. Your name is powerful. Your name protects us. We are called by Your name. Through Your name we can come before the God of Jacob, who is also our Father, in prayer. When we call upon Your name, You have promised to listen to us. In Your name, we have a relationship with God. In Your name, we have access to our Father, not because of who we are, but because of You. We can ask for help and for strength in Your name. We can ask for guidance and comfort in Your name. We can ask for forgiveness from our sins in Your name. We deserve very little, but You have given us so much. Our attitudes and our actions, our thoughts and our words are selfish and sinful and evil. But You came to give us new life and to cleanse our hearts and minds. In You, we can do all things. In You, we have the ability to do the good that we desire to do. In You, we have the courage to face new challenges and the desire to seek Your will for our lives. Without You, we are nothing.

Without You, we struggle and fail. Without You, our lives are empty, worthless, troubled, and difficult.

We can do all things through Christ who gives us strength! When we call upon Your name, all things are possible. When we rely on our own power and strength, we cannot succeed. Thank you for listening to us. Thank you for loving us. Thank you for forgiving us. Help us to desire the things that are pleasing to You and to live our lives in accordance with Your will. When we cry out to You, asking all things in Your name and submitting to Your infinite wisdom, You will give us the desires of our hearts and our plans will succeed. May Your name be honored and glorified in all that we do. We pray this in the name of Jesus Christ, our Lord and Savior. Amen.

Digging Deeper: What are the desires of your heart? How do they relate to the desires that God has for you and your life?

_____

_____

_____

_____

WORDS FOR EVERYDAY LIVING

When everything seems to be going wrong, You are always there to carry us through. When we have fallen, You reach out and pick us up. When we are weak, then You are strong.

You lived a perfect, spotless, guiltless, blameless, sinless life as our example. You gave of Yourself completely, fulfilling Your mission as our Savior. You emptied Yourself and lovingly died on the cross for us and our sins.

But You have overcome evil. Your goodness and love abound in the lives of the faithful. You have not forgotten the godly. You have not overlooked their cries for help.

Your Word is flawless. Your Word is perfect. Your Word is precious. It is a treasure for us to read and enjoy. It is a gift from God to be cherished.

Give us Your unfailing strength and courage. Guide and direct our paths. Make our way clear so we may see You. Shine Your love upon us so we are no longer weary and fearful.

Watch over me like a shepherd who watches over his sheep and protects them with his life. Guard me from evil and from the evil one who wants to drag me away from

You forever. Do not let my enemies or the pressures of this world overcome me.

We pray that Your love would work in our hearts and lives to mold us and shape us into the people You have created us to be. Create in us a new heart and replace the evil in our lives with Your good.

When we ask, You give us wisdom and strength. You have given us courage to face every challenge that comes before us. You know what we need before we even ask.

Only in You can we experience real peace and joy. Only You can fill the emptiness in our souls. Only You know what is best for us.

We should love You with our whole hearts and souls and minds. Our lives should reflect You. We are called to give an answer for the hope that we have. Give us boldness and courage to reach out in faith and share our hearts.

We need to be more like You. Take away the evil in our lives. Examine our hearts and show us where we need to grow.

You showed us how to live by Your perfect example. It is impossible for us to live a perfect life, but nothing is impossible for You.

When we are wrapped in Your love, You see us as perfect. The only good in us comes from You. Without You, we are nothing.

You are my Lord and Savior, the solid rock upon which I have built my faith. You are the cornerstone upon which I have built my life. You provide me with a firm foundation.

I need to trust in You and not rely on myself. I need a Father to take care of me. I need Jesus to be my Savior, and I need the guidance, comfort, and encouragement of Your Holy Spirit.

Teach us to rely on You completely for our every need. Listen to our quiet whispers and our cries for help and answer each prayer with Your perfect wisdom and timing.

Lead us not into temptation and deliver us from evil. Help us to flee from the temptations of the devil. He wants to devour us. He wants to destroy us.

You have blessed me with Your Holy Spirit to guide me in this world. You have sent Your Son to be my Savior and Lord. You have created this beautiful world for me to dwell.

Your way is not easy, but You have promised to be with me on every step of the path. When times are hard, You will give me courage to press on. I want to honor You with my life and with my work.

Although some people may gain the whole world, if they have lost their souls they will have nothing. The riches, wealth, fame, and power of this world are temporary. Only with You as our Lord and Savior will we have eternal life.

You are our rock! You are unchangeable, a solid foundation on which we can build our faith. You are our refuge! You are our hiding place. We need the solace and the peace that You provide.

Teach us to love and forgive unconditionally. We yield control of Your lives to You knowing that You are the potter and we are the clay. Make something beautiful out of our lives.

Help me not to be judgmental and condemning. Show me Your will for my life and help me to be a good ambassador for Your kingdom. Let Your kindness and love flow through my life and touch the lives of others.

Thank you for being our Savior. Thank you for being faithful, even unto death. Thank you for the gift of faith and everlasting life. Thank you for loving us today, tomorrow, and always.

Your grace is sufficient to meet all our needs, and Your love is amazing and never ending. You are our perfect and holy Heavenly father. Thank you for filling our lives with love, kindness, and forgiveness when we deserve Your anger, punishment, and wrath.

Purify our hearts and minds. Show us Your perfect ways and help us to live our lives in a manner that is pleasing to You. Take away our imperfections and the evil in our lives.

There is no one who is like You. No one can compare to You. Your majesty and power are displayed throughout the universe, and You have changed my heart! Thank you for Your life-changing love!

Your discipline helps us grow in our faith and helps to build our character. Your instruction helps us learn. Your love is revealed to us in Your Word.

In the midst of chaos, You provide peace. When we are uncertain of our future, we can trust You because You know the way. When we are tempted, You provide a way out.

When we cry out to You, asking all things in Your name and submitting to Your infinite wisdom, You will give us the desires of our hearts, and our plans will succeed.

SECTION 3:

Psalm 21-30

Day 61

O Lord, the king rejoices in your strength. How great is his joy in the victories you give! You have granted him the desire of his heart and have not withheld the request of his lips. You welcomed him with rich blessings and placed a crown of pure gold on his head.

Psalm 21:1-3

Dear Lord,

You are the King of kings and Lord of lords. You are the Alpha and the Omega, the beginning and the end. You are in complete control of this world and all the heavenly realms. You have given power to those who are our rulers. You have given strength to those who call upon Your name. You can do all things, and You will accomplish Your purposes here on earth in any manner that You see fit. Bless our leaders in government. Give them wisdom and guidance. Help them to stand firm in their beliefs and principles. Give them the courage to do what is right and to humbly serve You in their work and their lives. Give them the strength to fight for their convictions and the wisdom to know the truth and to follow Your path.

Bless our churches and our religious leaders. Help them to stay true to Your Word and to seek Your guidance in making decisions. Bless the time that they spend with You in prayer and in Bible study. Draw near to them, and give them the strength to shepherd their flocks and to lead Your people in Your ways.

Help each of us to acknowledge You and Your work in our lives. Help us to seek You first and desire the things that are closest to Your heart. Speak to our hearts, and show us how we can best serve You. Show us Your will for our lives and how we can accomplish Your purpose and glorify Your name in all that we do. Give us boldness and courage to share our faith and to honor You with our lives. You have given us many blessings and have promised us many more. Thank you for touching our hearts and drawing us to You. Thank you for the leaders You have put in our lives. Bless each of us with the precious knowledge of You, Your Word, and Your will. In the power of Jesus' name, we pray these things. Amen.

Digging Deeper: Do you pray for the leaders of our country and the world? Do you pray for the leaders within the church? Do you pray for your pastor or priest or rabbi?

_____

_____

_____

_____

Day 62

My God, my God, why have you forsaken me? Why are you so far from saving me, so far from the words of my groaning? O my God, I cry out by day, but you do not answer, by night, and am not silent.

Psalm 22:1-2

Dear God,

Some days we feel forsaken. We feel forgotten. We feel lost and alone. Some days we feel like nothing is going our way, and we are hurting. Sometimes we feel so far away from You. You are holy and perfect. We are sinful and flawed. You are almighty and powerful, and we are frail and weak. We cry out to You, but our prayers are not answered in what we deem an appropriate time. We want answers, and we want them now. We have no patience. We don't want to wait for Your perfect timing. We need help! We want it all, and we want it now.

Yet, God, You are patient with us. Sometimes Your answer is "No!" and sometimes Your answer is "Not yet." We realize that You know all things and You want what is best for us, but sometimes we aren't willing to wait. Sometimes we set out on our own, following our path and not seeking Yours. We get lost because we don't allow You to provide the light for our path. We would rather walk alone in the dark than wait for a lighted path to walk with You. We are stubborn. We are selfish. We are self-centered and self-absorbed. We need You more than we know and more than we care to admit!

Our sin blocks our relationship with You. Our sins lead us away from You. Our sin causes us to stumble and our eyes can't see and we lose sight of You. We have fallen and we are blinded! You have not changed, and You have not moved away from us. We are guilty and we are to blame. Forgive us, Lord. Help us to listen to Your voice and follow Your path. Lead us not into temptation and deliver us from the evil within ourselves and throughout the world. Show us Your will for our lives and guide us along the way. We ask these things in the name of our Lord and Savior, Jesus Christ. Amen.

Digging Deeper: Is there a time when you have felt far away from God? What caused you to feel that way? Why did Jesus quote this Psalm when He was on the cross?

_____

_____

_____

_____

Day 63

Yet you are enthroned as the Holy One; you are the praise of Israel. In you our fathers put their trust; they trusted and you delivered them. They cried to you and were saved; in you they trusted and were not disappointed.

Psalm 22:3-5

Dearest God, our Father,

You are the God of the Israelites. You are the God of Abraham, Isaac, and Jacob. You are the Holy One who delivered Your people from bondage and led them to the "promised land." You were with them day and night and provided for all their needs. Though they were rebellious, You continued to guide and lead them. You established a covenant with them and poured out Your love upon their lives.

You are our God. You have promised to take care of us and to guide and lead us. You have given us the precious gift of Your Son to show us the way. You have promised us eternal life through Him and His redeeming work on the cross. We can have a relationship with You through Your Son. As the Israelites cried out to You, so we can come before You in prayer and pour out our hearts to You. You have saved us from despair. You have given our lives meaning. You have filled our hearts with love. We have abundant life in You because You provide for all our needs. As we trust in You, we will never be disappointed. We will never be lost and alone. You have called us to be Your children, and You have promised to be our Father. You are the Holy One of Israel and the Father to us all. Thank you for taking care of us as a father cares for his children. Thank you for giving us blessing upon blessing. Thank you for loving us and forgiving us. Thank you for the gifts You have given to us in this life and for the blessing of eternal life with You, our Father. Thank you for sending Your Son, Jesus to pay the price for our sins. Thank you for Your forgiveness and for teaching us to forgive others. Let Your love and Your life shine though us today and always. In Jesus' name we pray. Amen.

Digging Deeper: What are some of the blessings that God has given to you for which you are thankful? Think of a time that you trusted in God completely and were not disappointed.

_____

_____

_____

_____

Day 64

The Lord is my shepherd, I shall lack nothing. He makes me lie down in green pastures, he leads me beside quiet waters, he restores my soul. He guides me in the path of righteousness for his name's sake.

Psalm 23:1-3

Dear Lord,

You are the good shepherd, and Your sheep listen to Your voice. Help me to listen to Your voice and to follow Your instruction. When You are in control of my life, I have all that I could need, nothing is lacking. You refresh my body and soul. You care about every facet of my life. You know when I need to work and when I need to rest. You provide strength and comfort for my weary soul. You have created a beautiful world for me to enjoy. Sometimes I need to relax and enjoy the majesty of Your creation. Sometimes I need to rest in Your loving arms. I need to rely on Your wisdom and guidance and strength.

You came to this world to show me the way. You came to guide me along the path. Your life was perfect, and You are an excellent example for me to follow. You are Almighty God, divine and holy. You chose to leave heaven and its glory to come to earth for us! You came to this world for me. You chose to give up Your throne, Your holy seat next to the Father to come to this world just for me. You willingly gave up Your life for me. You sacrificed for me. You lived for me. You died for me. You came to this world so I might have life.

You can guide me along the path because You have been there. You can help me with temptation because You have lived through it. You have showed me how to pray and the importance of prayer because You spent time with Your Father by praying. You have changed my heart and my life. Like a good shepherd, You laid down Your life for Your sheep. Thank you for calling me to be a sheep. Thank you for touching my life and for drawing me into Your kingdom. Thank you for calling me by name and for allowing me to call You by name. Thank you for loving me with Your life. Thank you for being my Savior and the Lord of my life. Thank you for Your life. In the name of Jesus, our good shepherd, I pray. Amen.

Digging Deeper: What does this verse mean to you: "The Lord is my shepherd, I shall lack nothing"? What is the shepherd's relationship with his sheep and also the sheep's to the shepherd?

_____

_____

_____

_____

Day 65

Even though I walk through the valley of the shadow of death, I will fear no evil, for you are with me; your rod and your staff, they comfort me. You prepare a table before me in the presence of my enemies. You anoint my head with oil; my cup overflows. Surely goodness and love will follow me all the days of my life, and I will dwell in the house of the Lord forever.

Psalm 23:4-6

Dearest Lord,

Life in this world is hard. There are days that are so difficult! There are times that we are walking in the dark and it is hard to see the way. Death and dying, sickness and disease, pain and suffering surround our lives. We have much to worry about and many things to fear. We can be overwhelmed by what is happening in our lives. We can be filled with despair and sadness, grief and sorrow. But, in all things and at all times, You are with us. We do not have to travel through the valley of death alone. We have You at our side always and forever. We are not lost and alone. We can rest in Your arms and surround ourselves with Your strength and love. You are with us every minute of every day of our lives. We need not fear, for You will provide for every one of our needs. You will comfort us and give us rest. You will wrap Your loving arms around us and carry us when we can't go on. Your power, Your strength, and Your wisdom are limitless and almighty. Our enemies will not overpower us because You have defeated all those who oppose us. We do not need to be afraid for You are with us today, tonight, tomorrow, and always. You fill our lives with blessings, our cups overflow. Your loving-kindness and Your goodness are gifts that You give to us. Your love is without measure. Your love is unconditional and perfect in every way. Although we deserve little, You have given us much grace. Your forgiveness covers our sins.

Although this world is filled with sadness and sorrow, You have given us the keys to heaven through the life and death of Jesus, our Lord. You have trampled down the gates of hell and defeated sin, death, and the devil. Nothing shall we fear. "Surely goodness and love will follow each of us all the days of our lives," and we will spend eternity with You. Thank you Lord! We praise Your name! We humbly bow before You and thank and praise You for Your blessings today and throughout eternity. In Jesus' name we pray. Amen.

Digging Deeper: What do you fear? How can the Lord help you overcome your fears?

_____

_____

_____

_____

Day 66

The earth is the Lord's and everything in it, the world, and all who live in it; for he founded it upon the seas and established it upon the waters. Who may ascend the hill of the Lord? Who may stand in his holy place? He who has clean hands and a pure heart, who does not lift up his soul to an idol or swear by what is false.

Psalm 24:1-4

Dear Lord, Creator of all things,

You carefully laid the foundations of the earth. You separated the land from the waters and created boundaries. You made order out of chaos. You spoke the world into creation. You set the moon and the stars in the heavens and put the sun in the sky. You started the world into motion. You made the rocks, the trees, the flowers, the animals, and You gave man dominion over all things. Your creation is beautiful and majestic. We fail to take care of this world that You have given us. We take the gifts that You have given us for granted. We aren't good stewards of the blessings that we have received. We don't take the time to thank the giver of every good gift, the Creator of this world, the ruler of all things.

O Lord, You are not only the Creator of this world, but our maker. You formed each of us as Your special children. You have blessed us beyond our belief, and You long to fill our lives with good things. You desire to spend time with us and to encourage us. You have given Your love, Your life, Your all to us. You are holy, powerful, mighty, incredible, awesome, and amazing. We cannot comprehend Your thoughts, Your ways or know the depth of Your love. We humbly stand before You. We are not worthy to be in Your presence. We are sinful. We are flawed, but You are complete. We need You, Lord. We have no right to stand before You or bow before Your throne, but You have given us access. You have given us forgiveness. You have given us an invitation. You paid for our salvation with Your blood. In You, the Father sees us as worthy; not because of who we are, but because of what You have done for us! Thank you for being our Creator and our Savior. Thank you for Your love and forgiveness. Thank you for listening to our humble prayer. We pray all these things in Your name, Jesus. Amen.

Digging Deeper: What are some ways in which you can overcome the sin in your life? Is there something that you are allowing to consistently block you from the relationship you desire with God?

_____

_____

_____

_____

Day 67

He will receive blessing from the Lord and vindication from God his Savior. Such is the generation of those who seek him, who seek your face, O God of Jacob. Who is this King of glory? The Lord strong and mighty, the Lord mighty in battle.

Psalm 24:4-5, 7

Dear Lord, our God,

You are the King of glory. The disciples wanted You to set up Your kingdom on earth and establish an earthly reign, but You are the King of glory. You are the king of heaven and earth. You are strong and mighty. You are holy and just. Your reign is everlasting. This world is temporal. You are not bound by time or space. You are not limited in any way. You are powerful. You are the King of kings and Lord of lords. There is no one who is like You. We are humbled in Your presence and awed by Your glory.

You have blessed us abundantly and loved us completely. You reveal Yourself to those who seek You. You answer the prayers of those who love You. You make Yourself known to those who look for You. When we seek, we will find. When we knock, You will answer. When we come to You, You heal us and make us whole. You complete our lives. You fill the void we have in our hearts. You emptied Yourself on the cross so that we may be filled and our lives may be full. Daily You show us Your mercy and Your grace. You never turn away from us, but so often we turn away from You. You have promised never to leave us or forsake us, but we often fail to come to You. We allow sin and evil to create a wall between us. We allow guilt and sorrow to destroy our relationship with You. You desire to give us good things. We often allow the bad things into our lives and our hearts. Cleanse us with Your everlasting love and purify our hearts. Replace the evil with good. Take away the ugliness and emptiness and fill it with Your goodness. Forgive us our sins and remove our sins far from us. Keep us from temptation and evil. Help us to do Your will and follow Your path. Be the King of our hearts and our Savior. In Your name, O King of glory, we pray to You. Amen.

Digging Deeper: Who is this King of glory, and what place does He have in your life?

_____

_____

_____

_____

Day 68

To you, O Lord, I lift up my soul; in you I trust, O my God. Do not let me be put to shame, nor let my enemies triumph over me. No one whose hope is in you will ever be put to shame, but they will be put to shame who are treacherous without excuse.

Psalm 25:1-3

Dear Lord,

You know me and You love me. You provide for all of my needs. You fill my life with meaning and purpose. You watch over me day and night. I trust in You completely. How I long to spend time with You. I need You every minute of every day. Without You, I am nothing. With You, I can do all things. You are strong and I am weak. You are my rock, my strength, my fortress, and my hiding place. You protect me from harm and keep me safe from my enemies. You shield me from evil. This world is filled with danger. The ways of this world are treacherous. The desires of this world are sinful. Help me to turn away from evil and desire the good that is only found in You. Help me to triumph over my enemies as You have triumphed over all things. Help me to trust in Your wisdom and strength and desire the things that You desire. I need to cling to You. I need to rest in You. I need to find hope in You. The world tears me down and draws me away from You. My sinful heart and the evil within me create barriers in my relationship with You. Please forgive me of my sins. Wash me and cleanse me from the evil that is within me. Help me to seek Your face and draw near to You. Let me not be put to shame and let me not bring shame upon You and Your holy name. As Christians, we will suffer much in this world as You have suffered. Help me to stand firm in my faith and never wander. Help me to be strong and courageous as I face the challenges of each new day. Carry me through when I can no longer walk alone. Provide for my needs so that I may persevere in my walk with You. Guide me along the path that I have been called to follow. Lead me beside still waters, and quiet my soul during difficult days and times. Give me the rest that only comes from You. Give me peace, the peace that passes all understanding. Let my hope be focused on You today and every day.

Unto You, O Lord, my God and Savior, my Redeemer, do I lift up my heart and soul. Thank you for Your unconditional love and acceptance. Thank you for Your complete forgiveness and loving-kindness. In Your precious name, I lift up all these requests. Amen.

Digging Deeper: Give one example of when your relationship with God has provided you a victory in your daily life. How did you overcome your sinful nature to follow God's path?

_____

_____

_____

_____

Day 69

Show me your ways, O Lord, teach me your paths; guide me in your truth and teach me, for you are God my Savior, and my hope is in you all day long. Remember, O Lord, your great mercy and love, for they are from of old.

Psalm 25:4-6

Dearest God, Heavenly Father,

You are the Creator of the whole world and my maker and redeemer. You have given me life on earth and promised me eternal life. You care about every aspect of my life as a father cares for his child, and You love me with an everlasting love. Your love for me is amazing. It is so deep that it is hard to fathom, difficult to imagine.

Show me Your ways, teach me to be the person that You created me to be. Help me to live a life that is pleasing to You. I pray that Your love would flow from my heart and that others would be drawn to You. I pray that You would use me as an instrument of Your peace and love to bring light into this darkened world. Shine in me and through me, and let Your light fill my heart and life. I want to share the faith that You have given to me. I want others to know of Your love and kindness. I want to be a witness to Your truth and share the hope that You have given me. Show Your tender mercy and love to me Your humble servant. Reveal Yourself to me and through my life. Send Your Holy Spirit to guide and lead me and teach me according to Your Word and Your will. Forgive me when I fail and gently guide me back into Your arms. You are always there for me every step of the way. Help me to remember Your great mercy and love and share those gifts with others. Be the source of my strength today and always. Thank you for saving me from myself, from others, from evil, and from my sin. Create in me a clean heart, O God, and renew and refresh my spirit so I can lovingly serve You. Thank you for Your unconditional love. I pray all these things in the name of Jesus, my Savior and Lord. Amen.

Digging Deeper: How do God's ways and His paths differ from your own? What is God teaching you now?

_____

_____

_____

_____

Day 70

Remember not the sins of my youth and my rebellious ways; according to your love remember me, for you are good, O Lord. Good and upright is the Lord; therefore he instructs sinners in his ways. He guides the humble in what is right and teaches them his way. All the ways of the Lord are loving and faithful for those who keep the demands of his covenant.

Psalm 25:7-10

Dear Lord,

You keep no record of our sin, of the wrong that we have done. When we ask You for forgiveness, You forgive us completely. You do not remember the awful things that we have done or the ways that we have hurt people and disappointed those we love, especially You. You don't hold our wrongdoings over our heads waiting for the opportunity to say, "I told you so!" or "I warned you about that!" You do not remember our rebellious ways or the sins that we have committed. Your love for us is perfect and unconditional. You don't hold back or withdraw Your love because of what we have done or haven't done. Teach us how to forgive others. Sometimes we say that we forgive them, but the forgiveness doesn't reach down into our heart. Sometimes we hold grudges against people. Sometimes we don't allow them to get close to us, so they won't be able to hurt us. Sometimes we forgive, but we don't forget. We remember how we have been wronged and we are cautious. We don't forgive completely, and therefore, we don't love completely.

Teach us Your ways, O Lord. Teach us what is right and how to love You with our whole hearts. Teach us how to love others and help us to pray for our enemies and those who hurt us. Heal our hearts and allow us to open up to others and let them into our lives. When we are hurt, we want to protect ourselves, and sometimes we shut others out of our lives. You have brought special people into our lives. We may miss out on the love and the blessings of knowing others. We were made to have fellowship with You and with others. Open our hearts to new opportunities and new possibilities. Help us to see others as You do, as Your precious children. Give us wisdom and guidance to walk through this life with You by our side, clinging to Your Word and Your ways. Help us not to be distracted by the desires of this world. Help us to seek You first. You are good and upright; forever faithful and loving. Continue to work in our hearts and help us to be more like You. Thank you for Your constant love and forgiveness. Thank you for never giving up on us. Thank you for calling us to be Your children. In the precious name of Jesus, our Lord and Savior, we pray. Amen.

Digging Deeper: Think of a time when you were hurt. Was it difficult to forgive the person who hurt you? Can you forgive and forget, or do you remember when someone has done something wrong to you?

_____

_____

_____

_____

Day 71

Turn to me and be gracious to me, for I am lonely and afflicted. The troubles of my heart have multiplied; free me from my anguish. Look upon my affliction and my distress and take away all my sins. Guard my life and rescue me; let me not be put to shame, for I take refuge in you. May integrity and uprightness protect me, because my hope is in you.

Psalm 25:16-18, 20-21

Dear Lord,

Sometimes the troubles and trials of this world are too much for me. I am lonely and afflicted, and some days I am completely overwhelmed. You are my Savior. You are my Lord. You are my source of strength. I know that the troubles of this world are only temporary, but they are great burdens on my heart. I need Your wisdom and guidance. I need Your power and strength. I know that in You and through You, I cannot only survive but shine. Help me to view every stumbling block as an opportunity to live for You and share the faith that I have been given. Help me to learn from the problems and trials and give me an opportunity to share Your love with those who are struggling with similar situations. Give me boldness and courage, wisdom and guidance.

I need Your grace and mercy. Sometimes I feel like I am alone and no one understands what is happening in my life. But Lord, You do, You understand every aspect of my life! You know my heart. You know me better than I know myself. You know when I am walking with You and seeking Your best for my life, and You know when I am trying to be a hero and walk along the path of life in my own strength. Forgive me when I am filled with pride and want to control all things. Forgive me when I am seeking the glory and honor for myself and not giving You the thanks and praise that You deserve. Forgive me when I have rejected Your ways and Your will to pursue my own plans. You know the plans that You have for my life! You know what is best for me. You have given me every good and perfect gift. You have blessed me beyond belief, beyond what I could imagine or think or even dream is possible. My life in You is filled to abundance. Guard my life and my heart. Rescue me from my sinful desires and evil ways. Protect me from harm and help me to firmly place my hope and trust in You. Be gracious and merciful to me, a poor sinful child of Yours. I deserve so little, yet You have given me so much! Thanks be to God for all that He has done! To God be the glory and honor and praise now and forever. In the name of Jesus, Your Son, our Savior, I pray. Amen.

Digging Deeper: What are the troubles of your heart? How do you seek refuge in the Lord?

_____

_____

_____

_____

Day 72

Vindicate me, O Lord, for I have led a blameless life; I have trusted in the Lord without wavering. Test me, O Lord, and try me, examine my heart and my mind; for your love is ever before me, and I walk continually in your truth.

Psalm 26:1-3

Dear Lord,

You know our hearts! You know our desires. You know our intent. You know the reason why we do everything. Sometimes, we want to give the glory and honor and praise to You. Sometimes our desires are selfish, and we want to receive the attention and the accolades. Sometimes we want to help others, and sometimes we want to look good in the eyes of others. Even when we try to do our best, we aren't perfect. We fall short of Your holy standards. We don't do what we should do, and we do the things that we shouldn't do. You haven't given us Your Word and Your commands to punish us; You have given us Your best. You reveal Yourself to us in Your Word. You show us Your will for our lives. You gently and lovingly teach and instruct us.

Being a Christian isn't about knowing all the rules and following them; it's about being in a relationship with our Savior and Lord. It's about walking and talking with our Lord. It's about trusting in You completely and surrendering our will to You. It's about acknowledging You before men and sharing our faith with those around us.

It's about spending time with You in prayer. It's about examining our hearts and minds and with Your help living a life that is pleasing to God. It's about asking for forgiveness and pouring out our hearts in prayer. It's about seeking the way, the truth, and the life that have been given to us by our Heavenly Father. It's about learning to love others as ourselves and loving God first and foremost. It's about learning to live without fear, knowing that God provides for all our needs. It's about living our lives by loving and serving God. It's hard. It's a struggle. Sometimes we are persecuted for our faith. Sometimes, there are stones in our paths, even big boulders that block our relationship with God. But God always provides a way for us when we seek his guidance and direction.

Thank you, Lord, for Your life and the perfect example You are to us. Help us to seek You and Your will for our lives. Examine our hearts and minds and lead us along the path that You have chosen. In Your precious name, we pray, Amen.

Digging Deeper: Consider a time when you were persecuted for your faith. How did God provide you with strength and redemption in that time of challenge? How did you continue to walk with the Lord when those around you tried to pull you off the path?

_____

_____

_____

_____

Day 73

The Lord is my light and my salvation—whom shall I fear? The Lord is the stronghold of my life—of whom shall I be afraid? When evil men advance against me to devour my flesh, when my enemies and my foes attack me, they will stumble and fall. Though an army besiege me, my heart will not fear.

Psalm 27:1-3a

Dear Lord,

You are the light of the world. You bring light and understanding to a darkened world. You supply hope and love to a world in need. You are our rock, our source of strength, our fortress. You provide shelter from the cold. You are our hiding place. We can seek comfort and guidance from You when the problems of this world become too difficult to endure. When we are overwhelmed and feel as if we can't go on, You are always there. When the mountains we must climb are too big and monstrous, You will carry our loads and our burdens. When problems weigh us down and sap our energy and strength, You have promised to provide for our needs. We can lay our burdens at Your feet. We can confess our sins and receive forgiveness. We can pour out our hearts in prayer and receive Your peace that passes all understanding. You know the answers even when we don't even know what questions to ask. You have paid the price by Your death on the cross and You are our salvation.

In You, we have perfect love and acceptance. There is no fear in love. We can hold on to You and You will save us...from ourselves, from sins, from danger, from evil, from temptation, and from enemies. We do not need to be afraid because You are the victor. We have You, the author and perfecter of our faith, to watch over us and guide us. There is no enemy that is stronger than You. There is no problem bigger than You. There is no evil that You have not overcome. Your goodness and mercy are abundant. Your love and kindness are immeasurable. With You by our side, we have nothing to fear.

Thank you, Lord, for providing for all of our needs and filling our hearts with Your love. Thank you for listening to our prayers and answering them in the best possible way. Thank you for the privilege of coming before You in prayer. In Your name we pray. Amen.

Digging Deeper: What are you afraid of? How can the Lord help you deal with your fears? What Bible verses bring you comfort and strength?

_____

_____

_____

_____

Day 74

One thing I ask of the Lord, this is what I seek; that I may dwell in the house of the Lord all the days of my life, to gaze upon the beauty of the Lord and to seek him in his temple. For in the day of trouble he will keep me safe in his dwelling; he will hide me in the shelter of his tabernacle and set me high upon a rock.

Psalm 27:4-5

Dear Lord,

In Your Word, it says, "Better is one day in Your courts than a thousand elsewhere." We need to spend time with You. We are uplifted and encouraged by worshiping You. We are filled with great joy and Your peace and love when we enter Your house and praise Your name. We are blessed by worship. Our hearts yearn for that special time when we worship You and praise Your holy name. We draw strength and wonderful insights from our brothers and sisters in the Lord. We need You and we are blessed by having fellowship with You and others. Your house is a holy place. We humbly come into Your presence and spend time worshiping You and bowing our heads in prayer! You have promised to be with us always! We can pray anywhere and at any time, but when we kneel before You in Your house, it is special! You have called us to remember the Sabbath day and keep it holy. We can do that by making it a habit to celebrate the Sabbath day with You and Your people.

Lord, You have promised to meet our needs and listen to our prayers. You love us so much! You watch over us and deliver us from evil. You protect us from our enemies. When we are troubled or in trouble, You are by our side to take care of us and carry us through difficult days and times. You have given us Your Word that is filled with promises and encouragement, insight, and wisdom. Help us to trust in You. Help us to seek shelter in Your arms and find refuge in Your house. Continue to provide for our needs and bless us abundantly. You are our God, our rock, our refuge, and our strength. Thank you for Your love and unconditional acceptance. Be with us and abide with us all of our days. Surround us with Your loving kindness and help us to share our many blessings with those around us. In the name of Jesus, our Savior and Lord, we pray. Amen.

Digging Deeper: How much time do you spend with the Lord? In His house? In prayer? In His Word?

_____

_____

_____

_____

Day 75

Hear my voice when I call, O Lord; be merciful to me and answer me. My heart says of you, "Seek his face!" Your face, Lord, I will seek. Do not hide your face from me, do not turn your servant away in anger; you have been my helper. Do not reject me or forsake me, O God my Savior.

Psalm 27:7-9

Dear Lord,

Thank you for listening to me and for hearing my voice when I call. You are gracious and kind. You love me with an everlasting love. You fill my mornings with sunshine and end my days with Your masterpiece written across the sky. You are our Creator and our God. You are our source of light and strength. You are amazing and all-powerful. You care about every part of my life! You help to heal the hurt. You give me boldness and courage to share my faith. You supply all my needs according to Your glorious riches! You give my life hope and provide meaning for my days. When I seek You, You will be found. When I ask, You answer. When I am lost, You lead the way. When I can't go on, You take me in Your arms and carry me. Without You, I am nothing. With You, I can do all things! You are my rock and my fortress. You are my hiding place when the world is closing in around me.

I know that You would never leave me. You have promised to always be by my side. Even when I feel lost and alone, I know that

You are there. Help me to seek You first in my life. Sometimes I wait to come to You until after I have failed miserably on my own. Help me to desire to spend time with You and to be near You. Help me to seek Your face and to seek Your best for my life. When I am on my own, I mess up and make a mess out of my life. Sometimes I hurt the people around me. Even when I try to do the right thing, it doesn't always work out. I need You, Lord. When others reject me and turn away from me, You are still there. When I come to You asking for Your forgiveness, You forgive my sin and wash me clean. You do not keep track of the wrong I have done. Time after time, You forgive me—not once or twice, but thousands of times. You do not hold my sinfulness against me. Help me to forgive others as You have forgiven me. Help me to not hold grudges or resentments. Fill my heart with Your love. Help me to forgive and to forget. Continue working in me, Lord, and help me to be the person You created me to be. Be merciful to me today and always! Send Your Holy Spirit to guide and lead me. I pray all these things in the name of Jesus, my Lord, my Redeemer, my Savior, and my God. Amen.

Digging Deeper: Have you ever felt rejected by your family or your friends? Have you ever felt rejected by God? What does God's Word say about His love and acceptance?

_____

_____

_____

_____

Day 76

Teach me your way, O Lord; lead me in a straight path because of my oppressors. I am still confident of this; I will see the goodness of the Lord in the land of the living. Wait for the Lord; be strong and take heart and wait for the Lord.

Psalm 27:11, 13-14

Dear Lord,

It is so difficult to wait! Whether we are waiting for test results or doctor's reports, we are waiting for a friend to arrive, or waiting for the phone to ring or the mail to come, it is so hard to be patient. Most of the time, we want things done our way according to our time schedule and our plans. We think we know what is best and how to achieve it. We don't want to be still; we want to be on the move. The world tells us that we need to look out for ourselves!

Teach us Your way, O Lord, and lead us along Your path. Help us not to be so caught up in our own plans and our own lives that we lose sight of You. You are perfect! We are imperfect. You are loving and kind! We are self-centered and self-absorbed. You are caring and compassionate! We are seeking our own desires and not Yours. Sometimes we want things for ourselves, even if it hurts others. We are sinful beings. We don't know how to love unconditionally as You do. We need Your help and Your strength. We need to seek You and allow You to work in our hearts and lives. You give us wisdom and strength. You can help us to wait and teach us to listen to You. Sometimes You speak to us in a whisper. Sometimes Your voice is heard in the thunder. Some days You grant us wisdom by reading Your Word. Some days Your knowledge is imparted to us through the words of caring and loving friends. You are always with us. When our enemies have surrounded us, You provide a way out. You are always there to take us by the hand and walk along the path with us. Your goodness and mercy fill our lives and touch our hearts. Your love provides for our needs. As we wait and we plan, be with us and calm our hearts and open our eyes. Teach us Your will for our lives and show us how to live a life that is pleasing to You. Help us to take our focus off of ourselves and our problems and look to You for all things. You are gracious and loving. Forgive us for wanting to do everything ourselves. Give us Your courage and Your peace. Help us to be patient as we wait for You and Your guidance. Thank you for Your love and support. We pray all these things in the name of Jesus who loves us more than we could know and who has taught us to pray. Amen.

Digging Deeper: How does God give you patience to deal with the worldly struggles that continually assault our spiritual lives? How can you apply the calm that God gives you to daily situations of stress?

_____

_____

_____

_____

Day 77

To you I call, O Lord my Rock; do not turn a deaf ear to me. For if you remain silent, I will be like those who have gone down to the pit. Hear my cry for mercy as I call to you for help, as I lift up my hands toward your Most Holy Place. Do not drag me away with the wicked, with those who do evil, who speak cordially with their neighbors but harbor malice in their hearts.

Psalm 28:1-3

Dear Lord, my God,

Thank you for listening to me. Thank you for hearing my cries for mercy. Thank you for answering my call and lovingly listening to my prayers. Lord, sometimes I don't even know what to say. I can hardly form the words as I cry out for Your help. I am overwhelmed. My needs are many. I pour out my heart to You even though I know that I am not worthy of coming before You. I am wicked, just like my enemies. My heart is evil and it needs to be cleansed by You. My thoughts are sometimes cruel and judgmental. I am filled with jealousy. My pride draws me away from You. I think that I am better than some people, but I am deceived. For all have sinned and fall short of the glory of God.

We all need You in our lives! We need Your healing touch. We need forgiveness and mercy. We need You to be our Savior and Lord. We can't save ourselves. There is no goodness in us, every inclination of our heart is evil. Only You are good. Only You can make us clean. Only You can wash away our sin. Lord, I know that on my own, I am a failure. I don't do the things that You have called me to do. I don't seek to do Your will for my life. I don't love my neighbors as I should. I don't reach out to others and share the precious gifts that You have given me. I do the evil things that I don't want to do. I keep trying, but I am weak. Lord, You are strong! You can do all things! In You and through You, I can be made complete. I can learn how to love and how to give. Help me to be a conduit of Your love. Help me to shine Your light in this darkened world. Fill me with Your love that it might overflow into the lives of the people around me. Teach me to forgive and to truly love the precious people You have brought into my life. Create in me a clean heart that can be filled with Your goodness and be rid of all evil. I lift up these requests in the name of Jesus, my Lord and Savior, who gave his life so that I might have eternal life. Amen.

Digging Deeper: How does God show you that He's listening to your prayers? How does He extend His healing touch to you during trials?

_____

_____

_____

_____

Day 78

Praise be to the Lord, for he has heard my cry for mercy. The Lord is my strength and my shield; my heart trusts in him, and I am helped. My heart leaps for joy and I will give thanks to him in song. The Lord is the strength of his people, a fortress of salvation for his anointed one.

Psalm 28:6-8

Dearest Lord,

What a privilege it is to come before You in prayer. You are worthy of our praise and thanks. You are my source of strength and encouragement. As I come before You, my heart is uplifted and my spirit soars. My heart leaps for joy when I am in Your presence. You shower me with love and kindness. You fill my cup to overflowing. You are my God and my Lord. You are my comforter and provider. You send Your Spirit to work in my life and to change my heart. You are so patient with me. Your loving-kindness is too great to imagine, too awesome to fathom. Your love is beyond words, it is truly amazing! You are the Creator of the world and my Heavenly Father. You are incredibly powerful and truly unbelievable! You take the time to listen to me and to hear my prayers. You do not judge me harshly. When I humbly come before You in prayer, You listen to me and You truly want what is best for me. You are patient when I fail, and You lovingly pick me up and help me along the way. When I am weak, then You are strong.

Lord, help me to look to You first for guidance and strength and not wait until I have fallen to get Your help. Be my shield and protect me from evil and the evil one. Be my fortress and protect me from my enemies. Be my hero and save me from the ways of this world. Help me not to fall into temptation. Remind me of Your Word and Your will for my life. Guide me back into Your loving arms when I have walked away and become lost. Thank you for being a good shepherd and for gathering Your lost sheep and returning them to the fold. Help me to listen to the voice of my shepherd! Thank you for Your unending patience and Your love. Help me to give You praise in every situation and for every aspect of my life. Thank you for being my Savior. In Jesus' name I pray. Amen.

Digging Deeper: How has God been your shield? From what or whom has He protected you?

_____

_____

_____

_____

Day 79

Ascribe to the Lord, O mighty ones, ascribe to the Lord glory and strength. Ascribe to the Lord the glory due his name; worship the Lord in the splendor of his holiness. The voice of the Lord is over the waters; the God of glory thunders, the Lord thunders over the mighty waters. The voice of the Lord is powerful; the voice of the Lord is majestic.

Psalm 29:1-4

Dear God,

Oh Mighty Lord, God of glory and strength, You are worthy of our praise. You are worthy of our adoration. You are worthy of all honor. You are to be worshiped now and forever more. You are holy and perfect, almighty and all-powerful. You are our Creator and Redeemer. You have a wonderful plan for us and for our lives. The heavens proclaim Your majesty. The beauty and wonder of creation display Your creative power. All of creation displays Your glory and strength. In You, the world was formed. In You, the animals were made and the flowers, the trees, and the plants. You spoke the mountains into formation and created the oceans and filled them with life. You made man and woman. You created us to have a relationship with You. You wrote Your law into our hearts. You have given us Your Holy Spirit to remind us of Your many miracles and the wonders of Your love. You have sent Your Son to show us the way and to restore our relationship with You. You have given us blessing upon blessing, every good and perfect gift comes from You. You are our Father, our teacher, our comforter, our sustainer, our Redeemer, our protector, our friend, and our confidant! You are worthy of our love! We are undeserving of Your abiding love and Your forgiveness. You accept us unconditionally, without limits and expectations! You are amazing! We are humbled and awed in Your presence. You are the King of kings and the Lord of our lives.

Help us to hear Your voice in the gentle rain and the wind. Help us to hear You in the thunder and see Your spectacular display of lightning. Help us to listen to the sound of the waves crashing to the shore and know that You are in control of all things. You have set this world into motion. You tell the sun when to rise and set, and You watch over us throughout the day and night. Protect us from evil. Guard us from what we don't see. Lead us along the path that You have chosen for us. Help us to listen to You and to love us all the days of our lives. Thank you for listening to our prayers. We ask this in the name of our Lord, Jesus Christ. Amen.

Digging Deeper: Has God ever spoken to you in a dramatic way? Are you more likely to hear His voice as a whisper or in the thunder?

_____

_____

_____

_____

Day 80

I will exalt you, O Lord, for you lifted me out of the depths and did not let my enemies gloat over me. O Lord, my God, I called to you for help and you healed me. O Lord, you brought me up from the grave; you spared me from going down to the pit.

Psalm 30:1-3

Dear Lord,

Some days we are in the pit. We are filled with despair, with anxiety, with depression, with evil thoughts, with hatred and jealousy. We are weighed down with burdens that are greater than we can carry. We are beaten down by the negative comments and weight of the world. The news each day can be depressing. There is much evil, anger, sin, sorrow, sickness, and sadness in this world.

Thanks be to God for providing us a way out of the pit and out of our despair. When we couldn't pull ourselves out, You sent Your Son to help us. We can't save ourselves, but Jesus can save us. He has defeated the wickedness and evil of this world. He has crushed the father of lies, our enemy the devil. He is even victorious over death. He died once for all men and paid the price for the sins of the world. Lord, You died for my sin. You died for me! You took my place and received the punishment that was meant for me. You were willing to sacrifice Yourself and give Your life for me. What greater love can there be? How could You demonstrate how deeply You care about me? You gave everything for me! Your love for me is amazing! It is incredible! You gave Your life so I might live!

You have listened to me and heard my prayer. You have provided for me day after day. You have filled my heart with Your love and have forgiven my sins. You give my life meaning and purpose. You have demonstrated Your love for me by suffering and dying for my wickedness and my evil ways. The grave has no hold on me, for death isn't the end. You have given us eternal life. We can worship You and be with You forever! We have been given hope from You, and we are no longer filled with despair. We have been lifted from the depths through Your strength and guidance. Thank you for cleansing our hearts of all evil and filling them with Your goodness and grace. Thank you for Your mercy and forgiveness and Your example of extraordinary love. Help us to be more like You! We ask this in the name of Jesus, our Savior. Amen.

Digging Deeper: Think of the most recent day that you've been in the "pit." What happened that distracted you from the calm that God provides? How did God reconnect with you during that challenge?

_____

_____

_____

_____

Day 81

Sing to the Lord, you saints of his; praise his holy name.
For his anger lasts only a moment, but his favor lasts a life-
time; weeping may remain for a night, but rejoicing comes
in the morning.

Psalm 30:4-5

Dear Lord,

You have filled our hearts with praise! Let us sing to You and
worship You in song. Let us sing our praise to the Lord. We need to
give You thanks and praise. You have touched our lives and blessed
each of our days. You are worthy of our adoration.

Lord, sometimes our lives are difficult. Sometimes the phone
rings and we are given terrible news. Sometimes the people that we
love are hurting. Sometimes sickness touches the life of someone we
know. There is death and dying all around us, and we are filled with
sorrow and sadness. Lord, You know our hearts. You know our situation. You know when we are hurting. You love us, and You listen
to our prayers. When we pour out our hearts to You, You are always
there to comfort us. You are filled with compassion. When we are
weeping, You are there to dry our eyes. When we are overwhelmed,
You are there to carry the load. When we are burdened, You have
promised to lighten our load. When we are guilty and overcome by
our sin, You have promised to forgive us when we repent and seek

You. When we pray, You answer our prayers in the best possible way. When we are weak and tired, You are our strength.

Help us to remember that sometimes joy comes in the morning. When the road seems dark and we are lonely, we need to draw near to You. There is a light at the end of the tunnel. Sometimes we need to take Your hand and walk with You when we can't see our way. We need to trust that You know us best and what is best for us. The troubles and trial of this life are temporary, our relationship with You is forever! You are eternal. You are the same yesterday, today, and tomorrow. You are our rock. You are our light. Let Your light and Your love shine in us. Help us to be a blessing to those around us. Thank you for Your loving-kindness. We praise Your holy name and ask these things in the name of our Lord and Savior. Amen.

Digging Deeper: Think of a time when you were overcome with sorrow or sadness. How did you get through this period of time? What can you share with someone who is going through a similar situation?

_____

_____

_____

_____

Day 82

Hear O Lord and be merciful to me; O Lord, be my help. You turned my wailing into dancing; you removed my sackcloth and clothed me with joy, that my heart may sing to you and not be silent. O Lord my God, I will give you thanks forever.

Psalm 30:10-12

Dear Lord,

You have changed my life. You have changed my heart. You have turned my sorrow and sadness into great joy. You have filled the void in my heart with Your love and transformed my life. You have put a song in my heart and given me a voice to sing Your praises.

Lord, thank you for listening to me and for hearing my prayers. Thank you for Your guidance and help in every aspect of my life. Teach me, O Lord, to give You thanks in all circumstances and in every situation. I know that You want what is best for me. You have blessed my life in so many ways. You take care of my needs, and You know what I need before I even ask. You have created me, and You know me better than I know myself! You can see into my heart, and You know everything that I say or think or do. You understand my motivation and my heart's desire. You know when I am putting on a show and when I am truly living out my faith. I pray that You would live through me! Help me to shine Your love and Your light to the world. Help me to be a good ambassador for You. Help people to see that You are the goodness in me. I am sinful. I am weak. I am fragile. I am needy. You fill me with Your love. You carry me when I can no longer walk. You lovingly provide for all of my needs. Teach me to praise Your holy name with my words and with my life. Help me to glorify and honor You in all that I say and think and do. Actions speak louder than words. Give me boldness and courage to live out my faith and let others see You in me. Give me the words to share with others to encourage them. Bless my words and actions as I share the faith and the love with those around me. Help me to trust in Your wisdom and power to open the hearts of the people that hear Your Word. Thank you for touching my heart. I give You all the thanks and praise and ask this in the name of Jesus, my Lord and Savior. Amen.

Digging Deeper: How has the Lord helped you and changed your life? What areas of your life still need to be changed for you to be a more effective witness?

_____

_____

_____

_____

WORDS FOR
EVERYDAY LIVING

You are the King of kings and Lord of lords. You are the Alpha and the Omega, the beginning and the end. You are in complete control of this world and all the heavenly realms.

Sometimes we set out on our own, following our path and not seeking Yours. We get lost because we don't allow You to provide the light for our path. We would rather walk alone in the dark than wait for a lighted path to walk with You.

You have filled our hearts with love. We have abundant life in You because You provide for all our needs. As we trust in You, we will never be disappointed. We will never be lost and alone.

You are the Good Shepherd, and Your sheep listen to Your voice. Help me to listen to Your voice and to follow Your instruction. When You are in control of my life, I have all that I could need, nothing is lacking.

Although this world is filled with sadness and sorrow, You have given us the keys to heaven through the life and death of Jesus, our Lord. You have trampled down the gates of hell and defeated sin, death, and the devil. Nothing shall we fear.

We are flawed, but You are complete. We need You, Lord. We have no right to stand before You or bow before Your throne, but You have given us access. You have given us forgiveness.

Help me to turn away from evil and desire the good that is only found in You. Help me to triumph over my enemies as You have triumphed over all things.

I want to share the faith that You have given to me. I want others to know of Your love and kindness. I want to be a witness to Your truth and share the hope that You have given me.

Teach us Your ways, O Lord. Teach us what is right and how to love You with our whole hearts. Teach us how to love others and help us to pray for our enemies and those who hurt us. Heal our hearts and allow us to open up to others and let them into our lives.

I know that in You and through You, I cannot only survive but shine. Help me to view every stumbling block as an opportunity to live for You and share the faith that I have been given.

Being a Christian isn't about knowing all the rules and following them; it's about being in a relationship with our Savior and Lord. It's about walking and talking with our Lord. It's about trusting in You completely and surrendering our will to You.

When the mountains we must climb are too big and monstrous, You will carry our loads and our burdens. When problems weigh us down and sap our energy and strength, You have promised to provide for our needs.

We can pray anywhere and at any time, but when we kneel before You in Your house, it is special! You have called us to remember the Sabbath day and keep it holy. We can do that by making it a habit to celebrate the Sabbath day with You and Your people.

You love me with an everlasting love. You fill my mornings with sunshine and end my days with Your masterpiece written across the sky. You are our Creator and our God. You are our source of light and strength.

You can help us to wait and teach us to listen to You. Sometimes You speak to us in a whisper. Sometimes Your voice is heard in the thunder.

There is no goodness in us, every inclination of our heart is evil. Only You are good. Only You can make us clean. Only You can wash away our sin.

Be my shield and protect me from evil and the evil one. Be my fortress and protect me from my enemies. Be my hero and save me from the ways of this world. Help me not to fall into temptation.

Help us to hear Your voice in the gentle rain and the wind. Help us to hear You in the thunder and see Your spectacular display of lightning. Help us to listen to the sound of the waves crashing to the shore and know that You are in control of all things.

Thanks be to God for providing us a way out of the pit and out of our despair. When we couldn't pull ourselves out, You sent Your Son to help us. We can't save ourselves, but Jesus can save us.

Help us to remember that sometimes joy comes in the morning. When the road seems dark and we are lonely, we need to draw near to You. There is a light at the end of the tunnel.

You have turned my sorrow and sadness into great joy. You have filled the void in my heart with Your love and transformed my life. You have put a song in my heart and given me a voice to sing Your praises.

SECTION 4:

Psalm 31-40

Day 83

Since you are my rock and my fortress, for the sake of your name lead and guide me. Free me from the trap that is set for me, for you are my refuge. Into your hands I commit my spirit; redeem me, O Lord, the God of truth. I hate those who cling to worthless idols; I trust in the Lord.

Psalm 31:3-6

Dear Lord,

I know that I need You. I know that I should cling to You and allow You into my heart. Only You can give me freedom. Only You can forgive me of my sins. Only You can redeem me. You are my refuge and strength. You are the solid rock upon which my faith is built. You can protect me from all evil. You can shield me from my enemies. You are real, and Your love for me is pure. Show me the way. Guide me along the path that I should follow. Lead me beside still waters. You are my Lord and my Savior. I trust in You.

Help me to worship You with my whole heart and not to be drawn away from Your presence. Help me to love You completely and not to love the things of this world. Help me to be satisfied with Your perfect gifts and not covet the things that others have. Help me to seek Your will and Your way! Send Your Holy Spirit to remind me of You and keep me close to You. I am sinful and I sometimes stray from the path that You have set before me. Sometimes I want to do things my way. I am distracted by the desires of this world. I allow other things to take my eyes off of You. I get trapped by the ways of this world. My vision is blurred and my priorities become jumbled. Help me seek not to please myself or to please others, but to live my life to please You. You have given Your life for me. Teach me how to live my life for You, giving You thanks and praise for all that You have done! You alone are worthy of praise! You have blessed us abundantly and given us every perfect gift. Thank you for giving us life. Thank you for showing us how to love and how to live. Thank you for carrying our burdens and lightening our loads. You are an awesome God, and we stand before You humbled and amazed!

Thank you for listening to our prayers. Thank you for Your loving-kindness. Thank you for the faith, hope, and love that You have given us. We pray all these things in the name of Jesus, our Savior and Lord. Amen.

Digging Deeper: Have you committed your spirit, your heart, your soul, and your life to the Lord? Why or why not?

_____

_____

_____

_____

Day 84

I will be glad and rejoice in your love, for you saw my affliction and you knew the anguish of my soul. You have not handed me over to the enemy but have set my feet in a spacious place. Be merciful to me, O Lord, for I am in distress; my eyes grow weak with sorrow, my soul and my body with grief. My life is consumed by anguish and my years by groaning; my strength fails because of my affliction, and my bones grow weak.

Psalm 31:7-10

Dear Lord,

Help me to always rejoice in Your love. Help me to see You and focus on You even when times are hard and I am overwhelmed by the troubles and trials of this world. You have promised to be with me always. You will not let my enemies triumph over me. You protect me from evil and from harm. Thank you for Your kindness and Your mercy. Thank you for comforting me in times of distress. I know that when I am weak, then You are strong. Your love shines through my life when I allow You to work in me. I know that You can do all things. I know that You are in control of everything. Sometimes, I think I am in control. Sometimes, I want to be in control. But I believe in my heart that You know, even better than I do, what is best for me. You love me with an everlasting love. You look at things from an eternal perspective. You understand things that I could never know.

I am weak and my strength fails. My body is weary, and I need You to restore my strength and my health. You are perfect in every way, and I am very human and frail. You can do all things, and through You, I can do all things as well. Fill me with Your Holy Spirit to work in my life and draw me ever closer to You. You are the love of my life. Help me to keep my eyes focused on You. During the difficult times, fill me with Your peace. When I am hurting or grieving, take care of my needs. Replace my doubts with complete trust in You. Strengthen my faith so I can walk with You. Help me to always seek Your will for me and my life. You have blessed me beyond measure. You have given me every good and perfect gift. Help me to give You thanks with my whole heart and with my life. Teach me Your ways, O Lord. Show me Your path. Guide me every step of the way! I ask all these things in Your precious name, O Lord. Amen.

Digging Deeper: Do you live your daily life with an "eternal perspective?" If you were more focused on God's gifts of abundance and less on the doubts that you harbor, how would your life be more richly blessed?

_____

_____

_____

_____

Day 85

But I trust in you, O Lord; I say, "You are my God." My times are in your hands; deliver me from my enemies and from those who pursue me. Let your face shine on your servant; save me in your unfailing love. Let me not be put to shame, O Lord, for I have cried out to you; but let the wicked be put to shame and lie silent in the grave.

Psalm 31:14-17

Dear Lord,

I do trust in You, but some days my faith waivers and doubts cloud my vision. I know in my heart that "You are my God," and I know that Your love for me is unwavering and unfailing. Sometimes I don't feel worthy of Your love and care. Sometimes I am focused on doing things my way. Sometimes my pride gets in the way. Sometimes my sinful nature ruins my relationship with You. Sometimes I am just stubborn. Sometimes I feel guilty for the many times that I break Your heart and let You down. Please tear away the walls that separate me from You. Soften my hardened heart. Open the eyes of my heart so I can see You and Your love. Show me Your tender mercies. Shine Your light into my life and let me see the love shining in Your face. Help me to run into Your open arms and not away from You.

As I stand before You, humbled in prayer, listen to my cries for help. Save me, for I am unable to save myself! I need You, Lord. I need Your forgiveness and my heart needs Your love. You know every aspect of my life. You created me and You know my innermost thoughts, dreams, beliefs and hopes. You even see into the darkened places of my soul. Cleanse me, wash me, make me clean. Take the evil, sinful desires from my heart and make me whole. Thank you for Your mercy and grace. Thank you for taking my sins and my burdens and paying the price for them. You received the punishment that I deserved. You suffered in my place. You poured out Your life for me. You died for me! What great love You have shown us! Teach me how to love as You love. Help me to live my life in loving gratitude to You, desiring to serve You and serve others. Your example of love is greater than any demonstrated in this world. Help me to shine Your light and Your love to those around me. Continue working in my heart and life and help me to be more and more like You. Teach me Your ways, O Lord, and show me Your path! I pray this in the name of Jesus who gave His life for me. Amen.

Digging Deeper: What doubts cloud your vision? What causes you to lose your trust in God or turn your eyes away from Him?

_____

_____

_____

_____

Day 86

Blessed is he whose transgressions are forgiven, whose sins are covered. Blessed is the man whose sin the Lord does not count against him and in whose spirit is no deceit. When I kept silent, my bones wasted away through my groaning all day long. Then I acknowledged my sin to you and did not cover up my iniquity.

Psalm 32:1-3, 5a

Dear Lord,

We need to confess our sins; they build up within us and create a heavy burden for us to bear. We need to repent and turn away from the evil that permeates our lives. We need Your forgiveness. We make many mistakes, more than we care to think about or admit. We try to hide the evil that is within us. We try to cover up the awful things that we do. We have terrible thoughts within our heads. How could we be Christians? We are so sinful. We know, Lord, that You came to this world on a mission, for a specific purpose. You came to restore our relationship with our Heavenly Father. You came to show us how to live and to give us life. You left the majesty and glory of heaven to humbly come to this earth. You came to serve...not to be served. You came to love...not to be loved. You came to suffer and die...not because You deserved punishment. You came for us... to atone for our sins. You came to pay a price that we could never pay. You gave Your life that we might have life in this world and the next. Because of You, we live! Because of You, we are forgiven. Because of You, our sins have been paid for and have been not only covered, but disposed of forever! You came to cleanse us from our sins and separate our sin from us. Because of You, we can have fellowship with our Heavenly Father who hates sin. You showed us the greatest possible love and You were willing to give Your life for us.

Thank you, Lord, for all that You have done and all that You are doing in our lives. Thank you for Your forgiveness and for taking our burdens on Your back. You have lightened our loads and renewed our spirit with Your hope. You have taken away the ugliness, the deceit, the evil, the guilt, and the blame. You have filled the emptiness and the void in our lives with Your love. You have given unselfishly and loved without limits. Teach us how to follow Your perfect example. Help us to rejoice in You and not to groan and grumble. All that we have been given is from You! We give You thanks and praise, glory and honor, adoration and love. In Your precious name, we pray. Amen.

Digging Deeper: Do you think it's important to confess your sins? Do you confess your sins to other people or only to God? How does confession heal your soul?

Day 87

Therefore let everyone who is godly pray to you while you may be found; surely when the mighty waters rise, they will not reach him. You are my hiding place; you will protect me from trouble and surround me with songs of deliverance. I will instruct you and teach you in the way you should go; I will counsel you and watch over you.

Psalm 32:6-8

Dear Heavenly Father,

Thank you for the privilege of coming before You in prayer. Thank you for listening to my prayers and for always being available to meet me where I am! You are my hiding place. Sometimes I am not ready to face the world with all of its challenges. I can't go out on my own; I need You beside me each step of the way. I am lost without You. I need You to show me the way. Sometimes, I can't see the path. Sometimes, I am not sure which way to go. Sometimes, I start out and lose my way. Teach me to trust in You. I pray that I would seek You and Your will for my life. Counsel me, guide me, and lead me in the way I should go. You know everything there is to know about me and You still care for me and love me. When the pain, the problems, the troubles and cares of this world are too much for me; You are always ready to carry my burden and lighten my load. You are so good to me. You are so loving and kind. You know what I need before I even ask. You are gracious and merciful to me. I deserve punishment and death for my many transgressions and my sinful ways, but You sent Your Son to take my place. He died for me and because He lives, I can live in this world and the next.

Don't let my enemies persecute me. Don't let evil triumph over me. Protect me from harm. You are my Heavenly Father. You long to hold me in Your arms and comfort me. You are ready, willing, and able to listen to my cares and concerns. Shelter me from the storms of this life. Give me answers to the problems that continue to multiply around me. Watch over me and keep me safe. Fill my heart with songs, and let Your love flow through me. I have so much to learn from You. It is my desire to continually grow in my faith. Grant me Your wisdom and guidance. Help me to make good decisions and to keep my eyes focused on You! Help me not to be afraid. Be my strength and my shield, my companion and my guide today and every day. I pray all of these things in the name of Your precious Son, my Lord and Savior. Amen.

Digging Deeper: How do you know if your decisions are right? Can you tell if God is leading you in one direction or another? When has God shown you the way?

_____

_____

_____

_____

Day 88

Do not be like the horse or the mule, which have no understanding but must be controlled by bit and bridle or they will not come to you. Many are the woes of the wicked, but the Lord's unfailing love surrounds the man who trusts in him. Rejoice in the Lord and be glad, you righteous; sing, all you who are upright in heart!

Psalm 32:9-11

Dear Lord,

You have created us to have a special relationship with You. You have given us the ability to think and make our own decisions. We are not puppets who are pulled by a string. We are not animals that are led by bit and bridle. We are human beings with the freedom to choose our own paths. Sometimes we choose to turn away from You and we try to do things our way. Sometimes we seek You and Your wisdom and guidance and strength. Sometimes we ignore You and we wander away from You, Your Word, and Your teachings.

How can the creation believe that it knows better than the Creator? How can the clay question the potter? How can the simple know more than the wise and learned? How foolish we are to turn away from our Heavenly Father! How prideful we must be to presume we know better than God! How arrogant we are when we think we have accomplished anything on our own! Lord, You have given us all things! You have blessed us beyond belief. You have given us a mind to think and a heart to feel. Yet, we often choose the wrong paths. We often make mistakes. We seek to do things our way and not Your perfect way. Teach us to be humble. Soften our hearts and take away our foolish pride. Help us to desire the best—which is Your best—for our lives. You are our Lord and Savior. You know us better than we know ourselves. You have shown us Your heart and given us Your Word. Let us draw wisdom and strength from You.

Thank you for the many times You have forgiven us when we have gone astray. Thank you for showing us the way and guiding our paths. You are our perfect example of love and kindness. Teach us to be more like You. You are able to forgive and forget. Help us to forgive others when they hurt us. Draw near to us each day and continue to work in our hearts and lives. Thank you for never giving up on us! In the name of Jesus, our Savior and Lord, we pray. Amen.

Digging Deeper: When has pride interrupted your spiritual life? How do you continually find ways to keep your own pride in check so that you can experience the full bounty of God's blessings?

Day 89

Sing joyfully to the Lord, you righteous; it is fitting for the upright to praise him. For the word of the Lord is right and true; he is faithful in all he does. The Lord loves righteousness and justice; the earth is full of his unfailing love.

Psalm 33:1, 4-5

Dear Lord,

As the birds sing freely and make beautiful noises, help us to also lovingly worship You. Give us an attitude of praise. Let our lives reflect the joy that You have given to us. Let our lips be filled with praise, and let our simple songs be prayers to You. You deserve all praise and honor. You deserve all the glory. Let our worship be pleasing to You. Let our hearts be filled with gratitude for all that You have given to us.

Thank you, Lord, for giving us Your holy Word, the Bible. You speak to us through Your Word. Help us to listen. Open our hearts and our eyes to see what You are teaching us. Show us how we can love You with our whole heart and serve You by reaching out to the people around us. Guide us according to Your precepts. Help us to see Your law as a gift and accept the instructions You lovingly give to us. You want us to seek You, and You have promised to make Yourself known to us. You want us to humbly come before You and knock at Your door. You have promised that the door will always be open to us and You will always be found. You want us to spend time with You in prayer and lift up our requests to You. We can share our joys and sorrows, and You have promised to carry our burdens. You are always there to listen. You are available to us each and every day. You are never far from us. Your blessings are new every morning. Great is Your faithfulness and love. Wonderful and incredible are the promises that You give us. You are worthy of our thanks and praise. You are an amazing God, and we are blessed to know You and walk with You. You have promised never to leave us or forsake us. We know that You are with us always.

Our God is an awesome God worthy of our love and praise. Thank you for blessing us with Your Word and listening to our prayers. In Your precious name, we pray. Amen.

Digging Deeper: Do you enjoy singing praises to the Lord? Do you prefer to sing praises in public or in private? How do you worship God?

_____

_____

_____

_____

Day 90

By the word of the Lord were the heavens made, their starry host by the breath of his mouth. He gathers the waters of the sea into jars; he puts the deep into storehouses. Let all the earth fear the Lord; let all the people of the world revere him. For he spoke, and it came to be; he commanded, and it stood firm.

Psalm 33:6-9

Dear Heavenly Father,

You spoke and the world began. You made the heavens and the earth and everything within them. You filled the sky with the sun, the moon, and the stars. You filled the day with the light and warmth of the sun. You set the world into motion. You filled the world with beautiful plants and a variety of animals. You created many wonderful and wondrous things. You made the land and the sea. You carved out the oceans and created the winds and the waves. You breathed Your life into man, and You made him in Your image. You created us to have a relationship with You. You are our Heavenly Father. As a father loves his children, so much more are we loved by You! We are blessed to have You in our lives.

By Your word, the world came to be. Creation was one of Your many miracles. As we look around us, the universe displays Your glory. The earth and the skies display the work of Your hands. You are all-powerful and all-knowing. You are the source of all miracles, and You continue to do miraculous things every day. Sometimes we try to explain away Your miracles. Sometimes we seek some rational explanation for Your divine work. Help us to see You and acknowledge You in this world. You are the King of kings, mighty God, our everlasting Father. You were before all things, and You are above all things. You are in control of all things. Touch our hearts and draw near to us! Help us to seek You first and honor You with our lives. As we admire the miracle of creation, we stand in awe of You. As we look at the majesty of the mountains or watch the ocean waves come crashing to the shore, we are humbled. You are mighty and we are quite small. We are insignificant, and You are truly amazing!

Thank you for caring about all of Your creation and for the incredible love that You have shown to us. Our God is mighty, and yet You care about every aspect of our lives. Thank you for the blessings You give to us every day. Help us to take the time to smell the roses and give praise to our Creator. In the name of Jesus, our Lord, we pray. Amen.

Digging Deeper: What impresses you most about the power of God? What part or parts of His creation draw you closer to Him? Are you ever filled with awe and wonder?

_____

_____

_____

_____

Day 91

The Lord foils the plans of the nations; he thwarts the purposes of the peoples. But the plans of the Lord stand firm forever, the purposes of his heart through all generations. Blessed is the nation whose God is the Lord; the people he chose for his inheritance.

Psalm 33:10-12

Dear Lord,

Early in the story of creation, the people wanted to build a great tower to make a name for themselves throughout the world. They were seeking the approval of men and not looking to God. They wanted the glory and honor and praise for themselves. But You confounded their plans and confused their language. Their plans were not blessed by You. The people were doing things their way and not seeking Your will and Your ways.

So often we want to earn the approval of men and are not concerned with the approval of God. We are filled with pride, and we want to make a name for ourselves. We believe that we have done great things, and we don't acknowledge our Creator who has blessed us with our skills and abilities. We think that we deserve the praise, and we don't give glory and honor to the One who made us.

Lord, You are eternal. You are timeless. You are without beginning or end. You are almighty and in complete control of all things. You know the plans that You have for each of us. Your way is perfect! Yet we often seek to follow our own path and seek to fulfill our desires. You have created us. You have chosen us and called us to be Your own. We ask You to bless us and guide us. We pray that You would show us Your will for our lives and bless the plans that we make. We pray for our nation for Your blessing and protection. We pray for our leaders that You would give them wisdom and guidance and the strength to stand firm in their convictions and live according to Your purpose. Your wisdom is beyond our comprehension, and Your thoughts are above our thoughts. Help us to seek You and Your blessings upon our lives, our families and friends, and our country. You alone are God, and we humbly submit to You believing that You can do all things and You are completely in control of every aspect of our lives and our world. Thank you for watching over us and keeping us safe. Help us to trust You with our whole hearts! In Your precious name, we pray. Amen.

Digging Deeper: Is it comforting for you to know that "the plans of the Lord stand firm forever"? What does eternity mean to you?

_____

_____

_____

_____

Day 92

But the eyes of the Lord are on those who fear him, on those whose hope is in his unfailing love, to deliver them from death and keep them alive in famine. We wait in hope for the Lord; he is our help and our shield. In him our hearts rejoice, for we trust in his holy name. May your unfailing love rest upon us, O Lord, even as we put our hope in you.

Psalm 33:18-22

Dear Lord,

In this world, there is much evil, much sadness and sorrow, and much sin. We need some hope! When everything around us is negative and the world continuously drags us down, we need strength. We need to be encouraged and have our faith renewed! We need You in our lives. We need to be in a relationship with You, not merely acknowledging Your presence, but trusting completely in You. We need to know You as our Savior and Lord. We can put our hope in You because we believe that Your love never fails and Your source of power is limitless. In You, we can do all things for nothing is impossible for You. Without You, we are lost and alone and doomed to failure. You are the one true source of our hope. You have given us hope and help in this world as we come before You in prayer with our joys and sorrows. You have also given us hope for the future. We know that Your purpose in this life is to restore our relationship with our Father. You took our place and paid the price for our sins. You gave Your life so we might have life and hope. You fill our hearts with Your love and in You our hearts rejoice.

Thank you for watching over us and keeping Your eyes upon us. When the world looks dark and ominous, You are always there to protect us. When we are exhausted and tired of fighting, You are there to carry us along life's pathway. When we are lost and alone, we just need to call out Your name for You are with us always! You are holy and perfect, and we are sinful and evil. Even when we are unlovable, You love us. Even when we are hurtful, You forgive us. Even when we are faithless, You are faithful and just. Thank you for never giving up on us. Thank you for Your complete, restoring love and forgiveness. Thank you for giving us hope. In Your name we pray. Amen.

Digging Deeper: What are some of the simple blessings in your life that show you that God is watching over you and protecting you? How do you show that you value these simple blessings to God and the people around you?

_____

_____

_____

_____

Day 93

I will extol the Lord at all times; his praise will always be on my lips. My soul will boast in the Lord; let the afflicted hear and rejoice. Glorify the Lord with me; let us exalt his name together. I sought the Lord, and he answered me; he delivered me from all my fears.

Psalm 34:1-4

Dear Lord,

As I consider the heavens a work of Your fingers, I am amazed. As I look around at the beauty of this world, I am in awe. As I observe the world in motion, I am so impressed. You are our Creator, and the world was formed and runs according to Your command. You are in charge of everything! You are King of the entire world! Your name is to be worshiped and praised! To God be the glory; great things He has done, continues to do, and always will do! You are our God! Your name is to be exalted. You are to be forever worshiped and glorified!

Thank you for loving us and for caring about every aspect of our lives. You are not too big or too great to be concerned about Your children. We can approach You. We can come before Your throne of grace. We can seek You, and You will reveal Yourself to us. You listen to our prayers, our cries for help, our pleas for mercy and forgiveness. You wrap Your loving arms around us and show us Your unfailing love! You fill us with Your love and shine Your light into our lives. You reveal the ugliness and the sinfulness in our hearts. You discipline us and show us the areas of our lives that need to conform to Your will. You have given us Your Word to guide and direct our paths. You speak to us and show us the way in which we should follow. You protect us and deliver us from the evil that is all around us. Your love drives out our fears and You gently erase our doubts. You have blessed us with every spiritual blessing and You care about our material needs as well. You have an answer to all of our questions if we would only seek You. You do not keep a record of our wrongs, but forgive us and love us unconditionally. We cannot earn and we do not deserve Your grace; yet You willingly give it to us in abundance. We are unworthy and You are praiseworthy. We are dishonest; You are fair, honest, and just. You are righteous and holy; we are sinful and unclean. In You, we are washed clean and completely forgiven. Thank you for Your unmerited kindness and love. Thank you for listening to our prayers. Thank you for the privilege of coming before You. We lift up these requests in the name of Jesus. Amen.

Digging Deeper: Generally, do you boast in yourself or in the Lord? Who do you credit for your accomplishments?

_____

_____

_____

Day 94

Taste and see that the Lord is good; blessed is the man who takes refuge in him. Fear the Lord, you his saints, for those who fear him lack nothing. The lions may grow weak and hungry, but those who seek the Lord lack no good thing. Come my children, listen to me; I will teach you the fear of the Lord.

Psalm 34:8-11

Dear Lord,

You have encouraged each one of us to come into Your presence and to seek You. You even ask the little children to come to You. You never turn away anyone who seeks You. You are always available to listen to us. You fill our lives with great joy, and You comfort us in times of trouble. You give us strength for each day and hope for the future. Your love is without limit, beyond our comprehension, greater than we can imagine. You pour out Your blessings upon those who seek refuge in You. You are a loving, caring Father who treasures and cherishes His children. You have given us a future. You have erased the ugliness of our past, and You guide us through each day. You surround us with Your love, and You have given us Your holy Word to show us Your will and Your ways. You are an amazing God. You are good and perfect, holy and pure. You are our Lord and Savior. You provide for all of our needs.

Your love for us is immeasurable. We are blessed to know You and to walk with You. You listen to our prayers. You are never too busy to guide and lead Your children. Teach us Your ways, O Lord. Show us Your will for our lives. Illumine for us the path that we should follow. Thank you for never giving up on us and for continuously showing us Your tender mercies. We deserve Your punishment and wrath, but You have shown us Your grace. You have shown us how to love by Your living example. You have shown us how to live by coming to this world. You know the difficulties and problems that we have in this world. You understand our suffering, because You have suffered for us. You are compassionate and caring. Thank you for Your forgiveness and love. Help us to listen to Your voice and follow You, our Shepherd. In the name of Jesus, our Savior and Lord, we pray. Amen.

Digging Deeper: What does it mean to fear the Lord? How can we both fear and love God? How does our attitude toward God affect our relationship with Him?

_____

_____

_____

_____

Day 95

The eyes of the Lord are on the righteous and his ears are attentive to their cry. The righteous cry out, and the Lord hears them; he delivers them from all their troubles. The Lord is close to the brokenhearted and saves those who are crushed in spirit. A righteous man may have many troubles, but the Lord delivers him from them all.

Psalm 34:15, 17-19

Dear Lord,

Thank you for Your promise to be with us always. When it seems like the world and its problems are closing in around us, help us to remember that You are with us. When we feel lost and alone, overwhelmed and burdened, You have promised to lighten our load and carry our burdens Yourself. You have not set us up to fail, You have promised to guide and lead us. You have not created us to be on our own, Your Word says that You will be with us always. We have been created to be in fellowship with You. We can walk with You and talk with You throughout every situation in our lives. You listen to us; Your ears hear our cries. You comfort us and wipe away our tears. You answer when we pour out our hearts in prayer and cry out for Your mercy. You love us. You want what is best for us. You care about every aspect of our lives. Your eyes lovingly look upon us. We are special to You. We have been created by You. We have been made according to Your purpose and plan. We have been placed on this earth at this time for a reason.

You heal the broken-hearted, and You renew our spirit. We can be crushed by the things of this world, but we have hope because You have overcome this world. We are not defeated when times are hard and troubles come upon us. You came to this world to save us! You demonstrated Your love for us by dying on the cross for us! You poured out Your life and suffered for us. What greater love is there? You were willing to lay down Your life for us. We certainly do not deserve Your love and Your mercy. It is a precious gift that You have given to us! When the world seems harsh, Your grace is sufficient for us. When the world seems cold, Your love warms our lives. When troubles abound and the way seems dark, You deliver us. When we are crushed and broken, You are there to heal us and strengthen our faith. We praise You, Lord, for everything that You have done for us and all the things that You are doing in our lives each day! You are a mighty God worthy of our thanks and praise. Thank you for listening to our prayers. Thank you for the blessings that You have given to us. Thank you for saving us from our enemies, our sins, ourselves, our temptations, and the evil that is all around us. Thank you, Lord Jesus. We lift up this prayer and the troubles in our lives to You! Amen.

Digging Deeper: What does it mean to be righteous? Who is righteous? How can you be righteous?

_____

_____

_____

_____

Day 96

Then my soul will rejoice in the Lord and delight in his salvation. My whole being will exclaim, "Who is like you, O Lord? You rescue the poor from those too strong for them, the poor and the needy from those who rob them."

Psalm 35:9-10

Dear Lord,

My soul rejoices in You! My spirit delights in You. I am encouraged and uplifted by being in Your presence. You fill my life with purpose and meaning. You bless me beyond belief. I need You, Lord, in my life. No one is like You, majestic and holy, righteous and just. You are strong and mighty. You can do all things. In You and through You, I can do all things. Your power source is unending. Your strength is amazing. You are an awesome God.

Your love surrounds us and completes us. You fill our cup to overflowing and continue to give us blessing upon blessing. As we share Your love with others, we are renewed and built up in our faith. As we worship You and draw near to You, You bless our hearts. You rescue us every day. We need to be saved, we need a Savior. We can't survive in this world alone. We need You, I need You! Troubles and trials in this world cause us to turn our attention on ourselves and they draw us away from You. During the battles, we need to draw closer to You and not turn away from You. When we are weak, You are strong. When we are poor and needy, You supply all of our needs.

When we think that we can do it all on our own, we are brought down and humbled because we need You. We can't do anything on our own. We are the branches and You are the vine. You give us life. We need to be connected to You in order to survive. You provide for all of our needs. When we have been severed from our source of life, we begin to die. Day by day, slowly we wither and fade. The life is drawn out of us because we can't live without our source of spiritual strength and our life source. When we are connected to You and in a relationship with You, You take care of us. You are the gardener. You are the potter. You are our Creator. When we are cut off from You, we are poor and needy and weak and lost. We have no hope and we have no life. We have a terrible void in our lives that can only be filled by You! Thank you for completing us and for loving us with an everlasting love. Thank you for forgiving us when we fall short. Thank you for picking us up and carrying us when we can no longer walk. Thank you for the many blessings You have given us today and every day! Thank you for being our Savior! We pray these things in Jesus' name. Amen.

Digging Deeper: What can you do to help the poor and needy? What gifts and blessings has God given to you to share with others?

_____

_____

_____

_____

Day 97

Your love, O Lord, reaches to the heavens, your faithfulness to the skies. Your righteousness is like the mighty mountains, your justice like the great deep. O Lord, you preserve both man and beast. How priceless is your unfailing love! Both high and low among men find refuge in the shadow of your wings.

Psalm 36:5-7

Dearest Lord and Savior,

It is hard to us to comprehend or begin to understand the depth of Your love for us. You are perfect, and Your love for us is perfect. We are deeply flawed and sinful human beings. Our love is marred; it is selfish, impure, and sinful. We cannot grasp a selfless, infinite, beautiful, complete, incredible love that is in no way earned or deserved. Our human nature makes it impossible for us to love perfectly. Your example of Your life and Your love show us how far we fall short of Your standard of perfection. Even when we try to do good and to love, we can't do it perfectly. We are selfish and truly evil by nature. The only good we can do is the good that You have put within us. We fail. We fall short. We do what we shouldn't do, and we don't do what we should do. We need You to cleanse us from our sinfulness and lead us on Your path. We need You to search our hearts and show us the error of our ways. We need You to look into the hidden areas of our lives and clean out the ugliness. We need You each and every day.

Even when we are unlovable, You continue to love us. Even when we are filled with evil thoughts and evil desires, You forgive us and create a new heart within us. Even when we fail over and over again, Your love amazingly restores us, and You take care of all of our needs. You are always faithful, even when we are faithless. You are filled with love for us, even when we reject You and turn away from You. You will always listen when we call upon Your name. Your unfailing love is always our source of strength and comfort. We can find refuge, protection, and courage in Your outstretched arms. You are always available to us with an endless supply of grace.

Lord, help us to be more like You. Help us to shine Your love into the lives of others. Help us to look to You in all times and in all circumstances. Help us to trust in Your perfect love even though we cannot fully comprehend its magnitude and strength. Teach us to be more like children trusting in their father and mother as we should trust in our Heavenly Father. Thank you for Your love and faithfulness. Thank you for listening to our prayers. Thank you for Your mercy and Your grace! In Your name we lift up our prayers. Amen.

Digging Deeper: How can you use the protection that God provides you to reach out to those around you who need that same protection? How can you share the blessings that God has given to you with the people that God brings into your life?

_____

_____

_____

_____

Day 98

Do not fret because of evil men or be envious of those who do wrong; for like the grass they will soon wither, like green plants they will soon die away. Trust in the Lord and do good; dwell in the land and enjoy safe pasture.

Psalm 37:1-3

Dear Lord,

Your Word says, "Do not fret" and "Do not worry!" You want us to live peaceful lives that are not filled with turmoil and anxiety. We cannot add a single day to our lives by worrying; actually worrying takes away from our lives and stress hurts us inwardly and outwardly. We are to trust in You. You know what is best for us. You created us, and You know us better than we know ourselves. Instead of trying to do everything on our own and being in control of matters that are beyond our control, we need to put our complete trust in You. Not just trust You with the little things, but with all things. Not just turn to You during difficult times, but at all times. Not just look to You for help after we have exhausted every other possibility.

Jealousy, anger, worry, resentments, and bitterness are all negative emotions that are harmful to our well-being. When we harbor a grudge, we are hurting ourselves more than the person with whom we are upset. When we are jealous, we are not being thankful for the things that we have. When we constantly desire more and more things, we are not content with what we have been given. You want us to learn to rely on You for all things. You want us to seek You first and not our own worries and desires. You want to bless us with good and precious things. Those things may not be the same as our neighbor's, but we need to trust that You know best! We are to dwell in this land and admire Your creation. We are to enjoy the blessings and the life that we have been given and not constantly desire more. We are to wait on You and Your perfect timing. We are to trust in Your will and Your ways and commit ourselves to You! Heal our hearts and bring to light the parts of our lives that need to be fixed. Let Your love fill the cracks and heal the flaws in our character. Teach us to rely less on ourselves and more on You. Thank you for allowing us to bring all our cares and concerns to You. You can do all things, and we can do all things with Your help! We pray all these things in the name of Jesus who taught us to pray. Amen.

Digging Deeper: What situations cause you to be anxious? What do you do when you are worried about something? What does God want you to do?

_____

_____

_____

_____

Day 99

Delight yourself in the Lord and he will give you the desires of your heart. Commit your way to the Lord; trust in him and he will do this: He will make your righteousness shine like the dawn, the justice of your cause like the noonday sun. Be still before the Lord and wait patiently for him; do not fret when men succeed in their ways, when they carry out their wicked schemes.

Psalm 37:4-7

Dear Lord, our God,

We are to delight in You! Some people think of worship as a chore, as a responsibility, as something they must do. But, actually, we have the privilege of spending time with You. Worshiping You fills our hearts and souls with blessing upon blessing. We are lifted up and encouraged by the time we spend with our God. Our faith is strengthened, and our spirits soar when we are in Your presence. We are filled with true joy and real peace as we humbly come before You. You have called us to worship so that we can be blessed, not as an activity to earn favor in Your eyes. You are our Father! We are precious to You, and You love us with an everlasting love. We cannot earn Your grace; it is freely given. We can't improve our relationship with You because You have called us Your sons and daughters. It is truly a privilege and honor to spend time with You...whether it is in prayer, in worship, in fellowship with Your children or in Bible study. During these times You teach us and draw near to us. We are blessed by You, and our relationship with You is renewed and refreshed. These are mountain top times, when we draw close to our Lord and Savior! These times help us as we go through the valleys and experience troubles and trials. You have promised to always be with us and to walk by our side.

Your Word says that we are to delight in You, and I believe that You also delight in us. You love us and want to bless us just as a parent wants to bless his precious child. You long to hold us and draw near to us. You want each of us to come to You and to know You. You want us to trust You and to be at peace. When trials and difficult times come our way, we need to commit these to You and allow You to work in our lives according to Your will. We need to be patient and to wait for Your guidance. Too often we jump into a situation without prayerfully seeking Your perspective. We can't just delight in You during the good times; we should desire to share all our times with You! Teach us to be still and know that You are God. We ask that Your will be done on earth as it is in heaven. Amen.

Digging Deeper: What are some of your "mountaintop times" when you have felt very close to God? What are some things that you could do daily to draw nearer to God?

_____

_____

_____

_____

Day 100

Wait for the Lord and keep his way. He will exalt you to possess the land: when the wicked are cut off, you will see it. Consider the blameless, observe the upright; there is a future for the man of peace. But all sinners will be destroyed; the future of the wicked will be cut off. The salvation of the righteous comes from the Lord; he is their stronghold in time of trouble.

Psalm 37:34, 37-39

Dear Lord,

You tell us that we should "wait" for You, but that is oh, so difficult. We don't want to wait. We want everything now according to our will and our plans. We want our prayers answered now! We want everything to go our way! We don't want to relax and wait for You and Your perfect way. We want to be strong and to do everything ourselves. We want to trust in ourselves and do it our way. You desire to have a relationship with us. You want to teach us to trust in You completely and wait for Your perfect timing! You want us to come to You with all our cares and concerns, all our troubles and trials, all our hopes and dreams. But we are impatient and we don't want to wait. Sometimes You want us to spend time with You and to be still and to listen for Your voice. When we allow all the problems and the distractions of this world to crowd our lives, we can't listen. We aren't tuned in. We are out of touch. We need to spend time daily talking with You. We need to be in Your Word. We should be spending time with You in prayer. We need to worship You and spend time fellowshipping with other Christians. By doing these things, our faith will grow and mature.

Our blessings come from You. Our salvation is a gift from You. Our righteousness comes from the Lord. We are not perfect, but when we are wrapped in Your love and bathed in forgiveness, we are blameless. We have hope, joy, peace, and love that come only from our Savior and Lord. Thank you for loving us and for filling our lives with goodness. With You we have strength and power. You protect us from harm and watch over us. Help us to trust in You today, tomorrow and always. You give our lives meaning and purpose. Thank you for being patient with us. Thank you for loving us. Thank you for listening to our prayers. Help us to listen for Your voice and teach us to trust in You completely. In the name of Jesus our Lord, we pray. Amen.

Digging Deeper: Are you generally a patient person? Is it hard for you to wait for specific things? How can you trust God to take care of your needs?

_____

_____

_____

_____

Day 101

O Lord, do not rebuke me in your anger or discipline me in your wrath. My guilt has overwhelmed me like a burden too heavy to bear. I am bowed down and brought very low; all day long I go about mourning.

Psalm 38:1, 4, 6

Dear Lord,

I have sinned. I have fallen short of Your standard of perfection. I have failed. I want to do good things, but my heart is filled with evil. I want to love the way that You love, but I am selfish. I am guilty and my sin is a heavy burden to bear. I am weighed down by my actions. I have hurt other people, even those whom I love. I have not been a good example to others. I want to do good things and shine the light of Your love to others, but my flesh is weak. My sinful desires corrupt my heart. I am evil although I desire to be a good person.

Lord, please take away the awful burden of my sinfulness. Cleanse my heart and draw near to me. Wash me clean and take away the evil that is within me. Help me to desire the things that You desire. Help me to be the person that You have created me to be. Be my rock and my fortress. Shine Your light into the evil parts of my heart and show me the truth. Show me Your will and Your ways. Teach me to be loving and kind as You are. Create in me a pure heart and take away the ugliness that is within me.

Lord, thank you for dying on the cross for my sins. Thank you for suffering on my behalf. Thank you for carrying my burdens and taking my sins to the cross. You are my Savior. You are my hero. You are my Lord and my God. Only in You can I find tender mercy and a heart filled with grace. You know me completely and yet, You still love me. You provide for all my needs, and You know what is the very best for me. Thank you for Your unconditional love and forgiveness. Thank you for Your kindness and acceptance. Thank you for always waiting to greet me with open arms. You do not condemn me for the wickedness that is within me. You forgive me and wash my sins away. Only in You can I find true love and real life. You are my Savior and I need You every day of my life. Thank you, Lord, for filling my heart with love and giving purpose and meaning to my life. Thank you for listening to my prayers. I humbly ask for Your forgiveness and mercy. I pray all these things in Your precious name. Amen.

Digging Deeper: Jesus' death gives us forgiveness for our sins. How can we use forgiveness in our daily life to draw closer to God and follow His Son's example?

_____

_____

_____

_____

Day 102

All my longings lie open before you, O Lord; my sighing is not hidden from you. My heart pounds, my strength fails me; even the light has gone from my eyes. My friends and companions avoid me because of my wounds; my neighbors stay far away.

Psalm 38:9-11

Dear Lord,

In this world there will be pain and suffering. In this world there will be conflict and strife. In this world there will be wars, death, and dying. In this world there is evil. Lord, thank you for coming to this darkened world and bringing Your light. Thank you for being a perfect example for us and for showing us how to live.

Lord, so many times it seems like this world is overwhelming and too much for us to handle. It seems like we are being beaten down and abused. Pain and suffering are everywhere. There is no relief. There is nowhere we can seek shelter from the storms of life. We feel like we are lost and alone. We are weary and burdened. We are hurting, and our lives are filled with groaning and sighing. Our eyes are tired from weeping, and our hearts are weighed down by our concerns.

Lord, help us to look to You, to turn our eyes to the heavens and seek Your face. Help us to seek Your promises and to read the Bible, Your holy Word. Renew our spirits and restore our strength.

Give us the words to say as we come before You in prayer. Teach us to trust in You and Your unlimited source of power and strength. Send Your Holy Spirit to comfort us when we are suffering and to guide us along life's paths. Show us how to live and how to persevere. Lord, You suffered and You were beaten and humiliated. You withstood great persecution for our sake. You came to set us free from the bondage of sin and the wickedness and evil of this world. You have provided for us a way out. You give us strength for each day. You have promised to never leave us. You have blessed us with every spiritual blessing. You provide for our needs each day and You have asked us to trust in You. Help us, carry us, and lead us through every day. Some days seem too difficult to endure. Some days are too much for us to handle on our own. But You have promised to always be with us. You can heal all of our hurts and our wounds. You can make us whole. Thank you for listening to our cries for help. Thank you for answering our prayers. We pray all this in the name of Jesus, our Lord and Savior. Amen.

Digging Deeper: When has your strength failed you? What did you do to renew your strength? How does God restore your faith?

_____

_____

_____

_____

Day 103

Show me, O Lord, my life's end and the number of my days; let me know how fleeting is my life. You have made my days a mere handbreadth: the span of my years is as nothing before you. Each man's life is but a breath. But now, Lord, what do I look for? My hope is in you.

Psalm 39:4-5, 7

Dear Lord,

You alone know the number of our days. You know the very moment we were conceived, and You know what each and every day holds. You know the number of minutes we have on this earth, and You even know the number of hairs on our head. You know everything there is to know about us. You have blessed us beyond belief. Your knowledge fills us with awe and wonder. You are all-powerful, all-knowing, and almighty as well as gracious, caring, loving, giving, and forgiving. You can do all things, nothing is impossible for You.

Lord, our hope is in You alone. We are nothing without You. We are lost in this world. Our lives lack meaning and purpose. But You, Lord, fill our hearts with love and fill our lives with blessings. You give us every good and perfect gift. You have given us life and blessed us abundantly. Help us to keep our eyes focused on You. Help us to live our lives seeking You and Your will. Help us to cling to You and to our faith when times get tough. Help us to remember that we are never alone. You have lived in this world, and You know the troubles and hardships that we face each day. You have promised to listen to our prayers and to answer them in the best possible way. Lord, please be our guide and show us Your wisdom and give us Your strength. Carry us through the difficult times when we can't walk on our own. Help us to remember at all times and in all circumstances that You love us. Your love and strength are enough for us. Your grace is sufficient. You are perfect and in You we are forgiven. We need Your love. We need You every day. Bring us back to Your loving arms when we stray from You. Restore our relationship with You when we have turned away and followed our own path. Remove the sin and the guilt from our lives and replace the ugliness and evil with Your precious love. Thank you for showing us the way. Thank you for Your forgiveness and love. Thank you for drawing near to us as we pray. We ask all these things in Your precious name. Amen.

Digging Deeper: What do you hope for? Where do you put your hope? Our life on earth is but a moment in time. Where will you spend eternity?

_____

_____

_____

_____

Day 104

He put a new song in my mouth, a hymn of praise to our God. Many will see and fear and put their trust in the Lord. Blessed is the man who makes the Lord his trust, who does not look to the proud, to those who turn aside to false gods. Many, O Lord my God, are the wonders you have done. The things you planned for us no one can recount to you; were I to speak and tell of them, they would be too many to declare.

Psalm 40:3-5

Dear Heavenly Father,

Thank you for the gift of song. Thank you for the opportunity to praise Your name and lift up our voices to You. Whether we are singing in a choir, walking through the park, in the shower, or humbly before You, we can worship You in song. You have filled our hearts with joy and through songs and praise and hymns and music; we can draw near to You.

As Your love bubbles over in our lives, we can share it with others. We can tell of Your glorious works, we can share Your wonderful ways, and we can proclaim Your holy name. Our lives are blessed by knowing You, and we can share Your love with those around us. We can share the love You have given us. We can tell of the many ways that You are working in our lives. We can speak of the hope that we have in You and the peace that passes all understanding. We are so blessed because of You. We have a precious gift that You have given to us, and we can share that gift with others. Sometimes we are afraid to talk to others about You. Sometimes we are fearful of being rejected or ridiculed. Sometimes we aren't sure what to say or how to say it. Thank you for sending Your Holy Spirit to teach us about You and to give us the words to say. Your Word is powerful! Your Word can change lives and can give life. Help us to share Your Word and to shine Your light. Help us to lovingly reach out and touch the lives of others. Help us to courageously share the love that we have been given. Help us to speak the truth in love and to share our hearts and our lives with the people that You bring into our lives. Let us be living, loving ambassadors for You in this world. We want Your name to be praised today, tomorrow and always. We pray for boldness and courage to share our faith. We pray for Your wisdom, guidance, and strength. We ask that Your Holy Spirit would use us to praise Your name in song, word, and deed. In the name of Jesus, our Savior, we pray. Amen.

Digging Deeper: Can you think of a time in your life when you were truly excited about something that God was teaching you or something that He did in your life? Have you ever been excited to share your faith with someone?

_____

_____

_____

_____

Day 105

Do not withhold your mercy from me, O Lord; may your love and your truth always protect me. For troubles without number surround me; my sins have overtaken me, and I cannot see. They are more than the hairs on my head, and my heart fails within me. Be pleased, O Lord, to save me; O Lord, come quickly to help me.

Psalm 40:11-13

Dear Lord,

Help us to focus on what is true. Help us to seek Your truth and Your Word. Help us to focus on You, the author and perfecter of our faith. When we get wrapped up in the world and the ways of the world, we lose our perspective. We get lost and confused; we are overwhelmed and overloaded. We don't have the strength to make it through the day without You. When we focus on our troubles, we can't see You. When we let the trials and troubles in our lives take over, we become ineffective. We can't live our lives for You when we are only looking at ourselves, our problems, our cares, our worries. We must seek You first. We need an eternal perspective. We need You. When we try to do everything on our own, we fail. We are miserable. We are burdened and heavy laden.

Our sins are huge burdens that we carry around with us. We need to get rid of the excess baggage. We can't continue to carry around the evil and malice, anger and jealousy, bitterness and hatred that fill our lives. We need to be cleansed. We need to be clean. We need to lay our burdens down. Jesus, You came to carry our burdens and take away our sins. You piled up all the sins of the entire world and carried them to the cross. The sins, our sins, were nailed to the cross with You and You took up our burdens and paid the price for our sins. Because of You, we have forgiveness. Because of You, we have love. Because of You, we are no longer burdened. Because of You, our relationship with God has been restored. Because of You, we no longer deserve to die. Because of You, we have eternal life. Because of You, we are free and we are able to rise above the sinfulness and evil in this world and really, truly live. Thank you for being our Savior and Lord. Thank you for living a perfect life and dying a perfect death for me. Thank you for listening to our prayers. We lift up our requests, our prayers, and our praise to You, Lord. Amen.

Digging Deeper: What excess baggage are you carrying? What are you missing in your spiritual life as a result of this excess baggage?

_____

_____

_____

_____

WORDS FOR EVERYDAY LIVING

Help me to love You completely and not to love the things of this world. Help me to be satisfied with Your perfect gifts and not covet the things that others have. Help me to seek Your will and Your way!

You love me with an everlasting love. You look at things from an eternal perspective. You understand things that I could never know.

Please tear away the walls that separate me from You. Soften my hardened heart. Open the eyes of my heart so I can see You and Your love. Show me Your tender mercies.

We need to confess our sins; they build up within us and create a heavy burden for us to bear. We need to repent and turn away from the evil that permeates our lives. We need Your forgiveness.

You are my hiding place. Sometimes I am not ready to face the world with all of its challenges. I can't go out on my own; I need You beside me each step of the way. I am lost without You.

Teach us to be humble. Soften our hearts and take away our foolish pride. Help us to desire the best—which is Your best—for our lives.

You are never far from us. Your blessings are new every morning. Great is Your faithfulness and love. Wonderful and incredible are the promises that You give us.

As we look around us, the universe displays Your glory. The earth and the skies display the work of Your hands. You are all-powerful and all-knowing. You are the source of all miracles, and You continue to do miraculous things every day.

Your wisdom is beyond our comprehension, and Your thoughts are above our thoughts. Help us to seek You and Your blessing upon our lives, our families and friends, and our country. You alone are God, and we humbly submit to You.

We need to know You as our Savior and Lord. We can put our hope in You because we believe that Your love never fails, and Your source of power is limitless. In You, we can do all things, for nothing is impossible for You.

You are not too big or too great to be concerned about Your children. We can approach You. We can come before Your throne of grace. We can seek You, and You will reveal Yourself to us.

You have shown us how to live by coming to this world. You know the difficulties and problems that we have in this world. You understand our suffering, for You have suffered for us. You are compassionate and caring.

Your eyes lovingly look upon us. We are special to You. We have been created by You. We have been made according to Your purpose and plan. We have been placed on this earth at this time for a reason.

Julie Walker Mitchell

Troubles and trials in this world cause us to turn our attention on ourselves, and they draw us away from You. During the battles, we need to draw closer to You and not turn away from You. When we are weak, You are strong.

Your unfailing love is always our source of strength and comfort. We can find refuge, protection, and courage in Your outstretched arms. You are always available to us with an endless supply of grace.

You want us to live peaceful lives that are not filled with turmoil and anxiety. We cannot add a single day to our lives by worrying; actually worrying takes away from our lives, and stress hurts us inwardly and outwardly.

You teach us and draw near to us. We are blessed by You, and our relationship with You is renewed and refreshed. These are mountaintop times, when we draw close to our Lord and Savior! These times help us as we go through the valleys and experience troubles and trials.

Our righteousness comes from the Lord. We are not perfect, but when we are wrapped in Your love and bathed in forgiveness, we are blameless. We have hope, joy, peace, and love that come only from our Savior and Lord.

Lord, help us to look to You, to turn our eyes to the heavens and seek Your face. Help us to seek Your promises and to read the Bible, Your holy Word. Renew our spirits and restore our strength.

Bring us back to Your loving arms when we stray from You. Restore our relationship with You when we have turned away and followed our own path. Remove the sin and the guilt from our lives and replace the ugliness and evil with Your precious love.

You have filled our hearts with joy and through songs and praise and hymns and music; we can draw near to You. As

Your love bubbles over in our lives, we can share it with others.

Our sins are huge burdens that we carry around with us. We need to get rid of the excess baggage. We can't continue to carry around the evil and malice, anger and jealousy, bitterness and hatred that fills our lives. We need to be cleansed.

SECTION 5:

Psalm 41-50

Day 106

But you, O Lord, have mercy on me; raise me up, that I may repay them. I know that you are pleased with me, for my enemy does not triumph over me. In my integrity you uphold me and set me in your presence forever. Praise be to the Lord, the God of Israel, from everlasting to everlasting. Amen and Amen.

Psalm 41:10-13

Dear Heavenly Father,

You are a merciful and loving God. Your grace abounds and You have blessed me beyond measure. You forgive me when I fail. I know that I have hurt others and have not loved them as You have loved me. I know that I am selfish and I seek to improve my situation and take care of my own needs instead of reaching out to others. I am not worthy to be called Your child. I do not deserve Your kindness. You reach out in love and accept me with all my shortcomings and failures. Although I deserve Your wrath and punishment; You shower me with Your mercy and kindness. Although I am sinful and sometimes evil, when I ask for Your forgiveness, You cleanse my heart and wash away my sins.

I have many enemies. There are many people who want to see me fail. There are those who seek to harm me and destroy my reputation. My desire is to serve and love You. I want to see Your name glorified and praised. I want to be a good example for You and shine

Your love and light into this world. I want to be in Your presence and to walk in Your ways. I want to draw near to You and draw my strength from You. You alone are God, the God of Abraham, the God of Isaac, the God of Israel, and the Lord of my heart. You are my Savior and Redeemer and You are my friend! You fill my life with meaning and my days with purpose. In You, I can do all things. Without You, I am nothing and I have nothing of value. Thank you for sending Your one and only Son to give his life for me; to be nailed to the cross to pay the ultimate price for me and my sins. Thank you for Your grace and mercy. Thank you for filling my heart with Your love. Please send Your Holy Spirit to guide me and show me the one, true way! Thank you for Your forgiveness. Thank you for Your unconditional love and acceptance. Thank you for being my Father. In Jesus' name, I pray. Amen.

Digging Deeper: These verses talk about integrity. What's the biggest thing that keeps you from being honest with yourself? How can your relationship with God allow you to become more honest in all of your interactions?

_____

_____

_____

_____

Day 107

As the deer pants for streams of water, so my soul pants for you, O God. My soul thirsts for God, for the living God. When can I go and meet with God? My tears have been my food day and night, while men say to me all day long, "Where is your God?"

Psalm 42:1-3

Dear God,

I need You in my life. I need to seek Your presence and spend time with You every day. Although I may not acknowledge this often, I long for Your presence. My need for You is greater than my need for air to breathe and water to drink. These can only provide physical comfort and strength. You fill my soul and replenish my spiritual strength. You meet all my needs, and You know everything I need. You know every part of me, even the dark places in my heart that I want to hide from everyone. You understand me and accept me. You love me even though I am unlovable. You have promised to never leave me even though I desire to hide myself from even You. You are my Creator and my Redeemer. You give me strength and courage to face each new day and every challenge that comes my way. When the circumstances in my life are too difficult to bear, You have promised to help me through and guide my path.

I need to spend time with You and allow You to fill me with Your love. Without You, I am lost and alone. I am weak and afraid.

I am self-centered and self-absorbed. With You, Your love and Your grace, I am able to reach out and share with others. You have blessed me and in You, I can share those blessings with others. When I am so caught up in myself, my problems, my circumstances, my life; I can't reach out and touch the lives of others. You have blessed me so I can be a blessing to others. You have given me gifts and talents to share with other people. Help me to keep my eyes focused on You and Your will for my life. Help me to shine for You and be Your ambassador. As the deer pants for water, so my soul longs for You. Fill the empty places of my heart with Your love. Renew my spirit and refresh my faith. Show me how to live for You. Teach me Your ways and cleanse my heart. Forgive me for my many sins, and allow Your light to shine though me. In Jesus' name, I pray. Amen.

Digging Deeper: What things of this world do you long for? What spiritual things do you desire?

_____

_____

_____

_____

Day 108

These things I remember as I pour out my soul; how I used to go with the multitude, leading the procession to the house of God, with shouts of joy and thanksgiving among the festive throng. Why are you downcast, O my soul? Why so disturbed within me? Put your hope in God, for I will yet praise him, my Savior and my God.

Psalm 42:4-5

Dear God,

My soul needs to be restored, refreshed, and encouraged. I need to be built up and prepared for action. Life in this world is a battle and my strength needs to be renewed. My focus needs to be changed. My perspective sometimes is a little off, and my priorities become mixed up. I need to spend time with You and to be in Your Word. I need to spend time in Your house and to worship You. I need to have Your people around me to keep me accountable and to encourage me to grow in my faith. It is very difficult to be a Christian in this world. When we are out on our own, our light seems to dim, and our hope is washed away. We get worn down and worn out. Our purpose and our focus become blurred. We lose our way.

We need time with You, God. We need to go with the multitude, with our brothers and sisters, to Your house. We need to sing praises, to pour out our hearts, and to share our love and our lives. We need to study the Bible, Your holy Word. We need to be taught and built up in our faith. We need to have our hope and our strength renewed. We need You! We are lost and alone without You. We stumble and fall, and there is no one to pick us up and show us the way. We need Your guidance. We need Your courage. We need Your love and Your forgiveness. We need to have our hearts made whole. We need to have our focus adjusted and our perspective changed. We need to have our souls encouraged and our faith restored. We can't do it on our own. Faith is a gift from You, and it is to be treasured. Please send Your Holy Spirit to work in our hearts and our lives. Please teach us how to live according to Your purpose and Your will. Work in us to make us the people that You have created us to be. Help us to love You and serve You with our whole hearts. Forgive us when we fall, and carry us through each day in Your loving arms. We pray all these things in the name of Jesus, our Savior and Lord. Amen.

Digging Deeper: Is worshipping God important to you? Is it a priority in your life? Why or why not? Do you think it should be?

_____

_____

_____

_____

Day 109

Deep calls to deep in the roar of your waterfalls; all your waves and breakers have swept over me. By day the Lord directs his love, at night his song is with me—a prayer to the God of my life. I say to God, my Rock, "Why have you forgotten me? Why must I go about mourning, oppressed by the enemy?"

Psalm 42:7-9

Dear God,

You have created the heavens and the earth. You have created the winds and the waves. The waters roar, the waves crash to the shore, and the tides roll in, all through the work of Your hand. You made the sun, the moon, and the stars. You have set the entire world into motion. You are in control of everything. You have inspired us with the awesome beauty and the majesty of Your world. You have made light for the day and darkness fills the sky at night. Everything designed exactly as You have planned, the entire world functioning in perfect harmony.

You have given us blessing upon blessing. You gently guide and lead us. When we walk with You, everything falls into place, and there is great order amidst the chaos of this world. As we wander off on our own and try to do things our way, the perfect harmony is ruined and the craziness of this world takes over. Nothing is easy without You. Nothing mysteriously falls into place. We messed everything up and wonder why things are going so poorly. We need You to bring peace into this hectic world. We need You to bring hope into this sinful world. We need You to bring joy into this world of evil and despair. We need You to bring love into this world of hatred, jealousy and bitter rivalry. You put the song in our hearts and the prayers on our lips. You create faith within us, and You guide us along the path we should follow. Your Word is a lamp unto our feet and a light unto our path. Your law and Your instruction guide us along life's pathway and show us how to live. Your discipline protects us from evil and from the things that destroy our relationship with You. Your loving-kindness fills our lives and renews our hearts and makes us whole. We need You to complete us, not some person to love us. We have been created to have a relationship with our Heavenly Father. We need You in our lives. Thank you for listening to our prayers. Thank you for providing for our needs. Thank you for being our Father. In Jesus' name we pray this prayer. Amen.

Digging Deeper: What is the song that is playing in your heart on a daily basis? Does that song reflect the faith that you have in God? Does it bring hope to you and those around you?

_____

_____

_____

_____

Day 110

Send forth your light and your truth, let them guide me;
let them bring me to your holy mountain, to the place
where you dwell. Then will I go to the altar of God, to
God, my joy and my delight. I will praise you with the
harp, O God, my God.

Psalm 43:3-4

Dear God, our Heavenly Father,

You alone are worthy of our praise and adoration. You are worthy of our love and affection. You are to be glorified and honored above all. Your name should be worshiped and praised throughout the nations. One day every knee will bow and praise Your holy name. You are our Creator and our redeemer. You have sent Your one and only Son to rescue the entire world. You sent Your Son to be a light to the nations and to teach us Your truth. You have revealed Your wisdom and Your great knowledge through Jesus, Your Son. In Him and through Him, You have revealed Yourself and Your love and kindness. You have given us Your Holy Spirit to continue to show us Your will for our lives and to teach us Your ways. We are like sheep that have gone astray. We seek what is best for ourselves. We are stubborn, we are lost, we are foolish, and we make bad decisions. We need a shepherd to guide us and guard us; someone to show us the way and lead us along the path. We need a shepherd that will carry us back into the fold when we have wandered away and will protect us from the evil ones. Jesus is our Good Shepherd. His love is unconditional and his kindness is without measure. He cares for his sheep each and every day and is always available to help, to guide, and to lead them. When we are lost and alone, He is there. When we have wandered away, He is there to greet us with open arms and carry us home.

Dear God, thank you for sending Your Son to us. Thank you for providing for all of our needs. Thank you for knowing what we need before we even ask. You are all-knowing and almighty. Your love is amazing. You are deserving of our praise. We deserve so little, yet You have blessed us in so many ways. We humbly bow before You. We worship and adore You. You are our joy and delight. We praise You before men and lift up Your name as we come into Your house. We celebrate Your goodness and Your mercy. Your grace is sufficient for everything we need. May all glory and honor and praise be given to You today and always. May Your name be forever worshiped and glorified! Amen and amen.

Digging Deeper: How does God's truth guide you? Jesus is "the way, the truth and the life." How does He impact your life? What role does He play?

_____

_____

_____

_____

Day 111

We have heard with our ears, O God; our fathers have told us what you did in their days, in days long ago. With your hand you drove out the nations and planted our fathers; you crushed the peoples and made our fathers flourish. It was not by their sword that they won the land, nor did their arm bring them victory; it was your right hand, your arm, and the light of your face, for you loved them.

Psalm 44:1-3

Dear God, our God,

As You have provided for Your people long ago, so You have provided for us each day. In the past, You brought Your people into the "promised land" and led them along the way. Today You have promised us heaven, a paradise for all eternity, our place to be with You forever. As You drove out nations and brought victory to the Israelites, so You have provided for our every need and given us victory over sin, death, and the devil. As our forefathers wandered through the wilderness in search of the promised land, You were with them. You gave them food to eat and water to drink. Your presence was real as You revealed Yourself to them. Today, You continue to take care of us. We don't see You as a pillar of fire by night or as a pillar of cloud by day, but You are with us always. We can come before You in prayer and lift up our requests and share our joys and sorrows. Your love is revealed in our hearts, and Your light shines through our lives. You have given us blessing upon blessing.

As the Israelites took for granted Your provisions and Your guidance, we do the same today. We fail to praise You for Your guidance. We think that we can do so many things on our own. We do not give You thanks for the gifts, talents, and blessings that we have received from You. We become filled with pride at our accomplishments and we fail to acknowledge that everything we have comes from You. You are patient with us and You were patient with our fathers. When we grumble and complain, You listen lovingly and gently remind us of all that we have. You do not turn away from us, but continue to forgive us and gently hold us in Your loving arms. You are willing to pick us up and carry us when we fall. You forgive us when we humbly come before You and ask. You cleanse our hearts and remove our sins. We need You and we seek Your face. Thank you for loving us in spite of how we act and who we are! Thank you for Your abundant grace and Your patience and forgiveness! Thank you for Your continued strength, Your abiding love and Your calming presence in our lives. Thank you for Your daily provisions. Thank you for listening to our prayers. In the name of Jesus, our Savior and Lord, we pray. Amen.

Digging Deeper: Does God lighten your path each day? How is He involved in your day-to-day decisions?

_____

_____

_____

_____

Day 112

You are most excellent of men and your lips have been anointed with grace, since God has blessed you forever. Gird your sword upon your side, O mighty one; clothe yourself with splendor and majesty. In your majesty ride forth victoriously in behalf of truth, humility and righteousness; let your right hand display awesome deeds.

Psalm 45:2-4

Dear Lord,

These verses in the Psalms describe You so beautifully. You are perfect, the most excellent of men. You have been anointed with grace, You are God's one and only Son. You have come to this world to show us Your truth. You left the majesty and beauty of heaven to come to this earth and serve man. Your mission was completed on the cross where You poured out Your life for us and our sins. You lived Your life on earth walking and talking with Your Father. You spent time alone in prayer. You asked that God's will be done and his purpose and plan for this world were made complete in You, in Your life and Your death. You knew Your role as a suffering servant and You gladly, willingly accepted it. Although You are the King of kings, You humbled Yourself and served all of mankind. Your perfect submission is an excellent example for us. We often look for the praise and glory that we feel we have earned in this world. We want all the good things that we deserve. We want to be recognized and rewarded. We want to be honored and exalted.

Lord, You were humble, even though You are God. You became a servant instead of a King. You showed us how we are to live our lives. We should seek glory and honor and praise not for ourselves, for our Heavenly Father. We should desire to see His name proclaimed. We should live our lives in gratitude to Him and all that He has done for us. Everything that we have is a gift from God. We have not earned and we do not deserve honor and recognition. We should give all glory to God. He is righteous. He is awesome. He is almighty. He is to be worshiped and glorified now and forever. We are but a small piece in this infinite puzzle. We are a small part of the eternal plan. We are very insignificant, but we know the One who knows all. We know the King of kings and the Lord of lords. We know the Alpha and the Omega, the beginning and the end. We can humbly come before the Creator of the universe because we know His Son. We can have a relationship with God Almighty because we know the one that He sent for us. We have been given life and faith. We know the truth and the way to the Father. We know Him who deserves all glory, honor, and praise. In His name we pray. Amen.

Digging Deeper: Life is often a large puzzle that we struggle to understand. How do you remind yourself every day to have faith in God's eternal understanding? How do you live out your place as a small but important piece?

Day 113

God is our refuge and strength, an ever-present help in trouble. Therefore we will not fear, though the earth give way and the mountains fall into the heart of the sea. God is within her, she will not fall; God will help her at break of day.

Psalm 46:1-2, 5

Dear God,

These verses from the Psalms are so comforting. You, indeed, are our refuge and strength. You are our rock, our mighty fortress, our pillar of strength. If You are for us, who can be against us? If You are watching over us, we have nothing to fear. With Your support and encouragement, we can do all things. No matter what trouble comes to us, no matter what trials come before us, no matter what problems we face, we know that You are with us. You can do all things! You alone are God. There is no one like You. There is nothing to fear. Your perfect love drives out all fear. When we are weak and our faith is weakened, we are afraid, we fall into despair. When we allow You to be in control of our lives and to provide for our needs, we are blessed. We have everything that we could ever need. We will not be crushed or battered or bruised, for You are with us. When we fall, You help us. When we fail and we do not have the strength to continue, You carry us. You pick us up and hold us in Your loving arms. You restore our strength and fulfill our needs and show us the way.

When the world comes crashing down around us, we do not need to fear. When the crisis seems too big and the problems overwhelming, we need to cling to You and Your love. Nothing is impossible for You. Nothing is too big for You. Nothing is overwhelming for You.

We need to learn to trust and to believe in Your infinite ability and almighty power. We can rest assured that in Your arms we are safe and secure. You love us more than our earthly father or mother ever could. You are truly an awesome God. We need You every minute of every day. On our own, we fall short, we fail, we are human and we make mistakes. We are powerless and we are small. We sometimes think that we are in control and we can do things our way, but we are wrong. We are often deceived. We lose our way, we miss the mark, we aren't perfect. But You are perfect! You have an unlimited source of power, strength, wisdom, guidance, love, peace, and forgiveness. We can never measure up, but You are willing to forgive our failures and take away our sins. You love us completely. Thank you, Lord. We humbly come before You in prayer in the name of Jesus, Your Son and our Savior. Amen.

Digging Deeper: Who is your rock, your refuge, your source of strength? Do you have a friend or a family member that you turn to in times of need? How does Jesus fill that role in your life?

Day 114

Be still, and know that I am God; I will be exalted among the nations, I will be exalted in the earth. The Lord Almighty is with us; the God of Jacob is our fortress.

Psalm 46:10-11

Dear Lord,

We need to hear these verses. We need to be still and to know that You are God. Our world is so chaotic. We get so busy. We get bogged down in this fast-paced world. We get easily distracted and totally overloaded. We try to do so much and cram so many things into our days. We run and we run and sometimes we don't seem to go anywhere or get anything done. We hurry, we race, and we pile more and more on our plates. We don't want to let people down. We can't say "no." We take on more responsibilities when we can't handle what we have. We try to do everything, and we end up doing nothing very well. We go and we go and we go until we can't go anymore.

Lord, You know what life is like in this world. Sometimes You would take a time-out from the people, the pressures, the responsibilities, and You would spend time alone with Your Father. You needed time away to renew Your mind and restore Your strength and readjust Your focus. How much more do we need that special time? You commanded us to "remember the Sabbath and keep it holy." We need some peace and quiet. We need time to reflect and prioritize our lives. We need to spend time with You. We need Your strength, Your wisdom, Your guidance, and Your peace. Without You, our lives are in complete chaos. Without You, our batteries cannot be recharged. Without You, our source of power runs dry. Without You, we can't do anything. With You, we can do all things.

Help us to put our lives in order. Teach us to seek You first, and allow You to work in our hearts. Show us how we can live in this crazy world and find Your peace that passes all understanding. Speak to our hearts and quiet our souls. Help us to make good decisions and look to You first to guide us along life's path. We ask all these things in Jesus' name. Amen.

Digging Deeper: When are you still before God? Do you take time to listen to Him, or do you just talk to Him? Do you observe a Sabbath rest?

_____

_____

_____

_____

Day 115

How awesome is the Lord Most High, the great King over all the earth! He subdued nations under us, peoples under our feet. For God is the King of all the earth; sing to him a psalm of praise. God reigns over the nations; God is seated on his holy throne.

Psalm 47:2-3, 7-8

Dear God,

You are worthy of our praise and adoration. We sometimes take You for granted. We don't stop to marvel at the work of Your creation. We don't take the time to look at the beauty of our surroundings. We don't rest in Your presence or admire the works of Your hands. You are awesome! You created the heavens and the earth, the light and the darkness, the water and the land, all the trees and the flowers, the birds and the fish and the animals. Then You made man in Your own image. You created us to have a relationship with You and with Your creation. You chose us to rule over this world and live in peace and harmony with this world. But we are sinful and selfish. We want things our way. We don't want to follow Your rules, Your laws, Your commandments; we prefer to do things our own way. Instead of living in harmony, things are out of balance. Our priorities aren't in order, our lives are chaotic, and things are out of control. We need You to reign in our hearts, in our lives, and in this world. We need You to be on the throne and in complete control. We need

You to be the King of all the earth and the Lord of our lives. We can't do things on our own. We aren't living in peace with ourselves, our neighbors, our world or our God. We need to adjust our focus and spend time worshiping You and not ourselves and our abilities. Everything we have been given has been a gift from You. You deserve the glory and honor; we, certainly, do not. You are worthy of our praise and our love. You have loved us with an everlasting love and shown us how to love each other. We need You and Your perfect example. We need You and Your compassion. We need Your forgiveness to restore our relationship with You and with others. We need to be healed because we are broken and there is no peace within us. Only You can give us real, true peace. Only in You can we be made whole. Only with You can we find purpose and meaning, understanding and wisdom. Thank you for never giving up on us and for showering us with Your love and Your blessings. Forgive us our sins and help us to become the people that You have created us to be. We ask these things in the name of Jesus, our Lord and Savior. Amen.

Digging Deeper: Our God is an awesome God! How do you explain that to someone who does not know Him? What other descriptive words do you like to use to describe God?

Day 116

Great is the Lord, and most worthy of praise, in the city of our God, his holy mountain. Within your temple, O God, we meditate on your unfailing love. Like your name, O God, your praise reaches to the ends of the earth; your right hand is filled with righteousness.

Psalm 48:1, 9-10

Dear God,

As we bow down to worship You and to draw near to You, we are humbled. We are merely Your servants; we are unworthy to come before You. You are an awesome God, truly amazing, full of compassion and grace, You are loving and kind. Your name is to be praised and glorified. You are eternal and Your love is everlasting. The works of Your hands are inspiring. Your creation is filled with wonder, beauty, and majesty. As we look out into the world or up into the heavens, we see evidence of Your wondrous creation. The mountains proclaim Your majesty; the sun and the starry skies shine Your light; the seas are teeming with all varieties of fish, plants, and animals. Even the wind and the waves obey You. The sun rises and sets at Your command. You are in control of all things.

Lord, You are truly great and worthy of our love, our thanks, and our praise. Thank you for giving us a place to worship You. As we go into Your house for worship, we know that You are always there to welcome us and greet us. You meet us and You meet our needs. As we come to worship You, we are blessed, and we are filled with Your Holy Spirit. You encourage us through Your Word, and You speak directly to our hearts. We can worship You in church, in our homes, in nature, on vacation, and as we walk through our daily lives. You listen when we call. You answer our prayers. You provide for our needs. You forgive us when we ask. You gave Your life for us. You have restored our broken relationships and filled the void in our lives. You have given us meaning and purpose. You strengthen our faith and surround us with Your love. You are truly awesome and incredible. You are our perfect example and our one true hope. Although we are unworthy, You have called us Your children and gathered us into Your arms. Although we are sinful, You have forgiven us and washed away all the ugliness and evil in our lives. Although we are weak, we are made strong in Your power. Although we struggle in this life, You are always there to guide us along the path and show us the way. Humbly we bow before You and lift up our requests to You. Thank you for listening to our prayers and lovingly answering our requests. In Your precious name, dear Lord, we pray. Amen.

Digging Deeper: Do you meditate on God's Word or do you just read the Bible? Does God speak to you in His Word?

_____

_____

_____

_____

Day 117

Hear this, all you peoples; listen, all who live in this world, both low and high, rich and poor alike... No man can redeem the life of another or give to God a ransom for him—the ransom for a life is costly, no payment is ever enough—that he should live on forever and not see decay.

Psalm 49:1-2, 7-8

Dear Heavenly Father,

You have created each person in this world at this specific time according to Your Almighty purpose. You are in control of all things. You are God, You are perfect, You are holy, and You are righteous. You made all people: the rich and the poor, the strong and the weak, the healthy and the sick, the wise and the foolish. We are all Your creation, all people everywhere in the world. Each life is precious to You. Each person is a work of Your hands. Each child is a gift from heaven. It is Your desire that all people be saved. You want to be the Heavenly Father for all people of all nations. You want to have a relationship with the people that You have brought into this world. You want to love and care for everyone.

You love us so much that You sent Your Son to pay the price for our sins. You sent Your Son to live a perfect life and die a perfect death. We cannot atone for our sins. We cannot pay for the wrongs that we have done. We cannot be perfect. We cannot live up to Your holy and righteous standards. We fall short. We don't measure up.

We fail each and every day. We need a Savior. We need someone to help us along the way. We need someone to restore our broken relationship with our Father. We can't pay the ransom for our own lives or for anyone else. Because of our sins, we deserve to be punished. We deserve to die. We deserve to be condemned. But Your love for us is so great, You sent Your Son to pay the price for us. He was the ransom. He was the scapegoat. He was the perfect sacrifice. He willingly chose the road of suffering because of His love for us. We do not deserve mercy and grace. We deserve the wrath of God. But You have chosen to bless us with an abundance of love. Your Son piled the sins of the world on his back and carried the weight of our burdens to the cross. There is no greater example of love. Thank you for the unbelievable gifts of forgiveness, mercy, and compassion. Thank you for sending Your Son to take our place and to make atonement for our sins. All glory and thanks be given to God for his indescribable gift. In Jesus' name we pray. Amen.

Digging Deeper: Why did Jesus need to die on the cross? Do you believe that He died for you and your sins?

_____

_____

_____

Day 118

The Mighty One, God, the Lord, speaks and summons the earth from the rising of the sun to the place where it sets. From Zion, perfect in beauty, God shines forth. He summons the heavens above, and the earth, that he may judge his people.

Psalm 50:1-2, 4

Dear God,

The heavens cry out and proclaim Your beauty and majesty. The stars sparkle in the skies at night and shine Your light. The sun rises in the morning and sets in the evening according to Your schedule, according to Your plans. You are in control of all things. You put this world into motion, and You are watching over us and taking care of us every day. You love us more than we could ever know or imagine. You have blessed us with every spiritual blessing. You shine Your light into our hearts and You desire to share Your blessings with all people. You want to give to us every good and perfect gift. You want to fill our lives with Your love and everlasting kindness. You want to draw near to us and to work in our hearts and our lives! You are the King of kings and the Lord of lords, but You take the time to care about each one of us. You want to love each of us, Your precious creation, as a father loves his children.

We have done nothing to earn or deserve Your love. We are not worthy of Your kindness. We constantly disappoint You. We don't do the things we should do, and we do the things that we shouldn't do. We try, but we fail. We want to do good things, but we often do evil. We want to love You, but we can't do it perfectly. We deserve Your punishment and Your judgment, but we need Your healing touch. We need forgiveness. We need to be washed clean. We need Your saving grace. We need You to cleanse our hearts and to be made pure. You are our Heavenly Father and we need Your love. We cling to the promises You have given us: Your promises to never leave us or forsake us, Your promises to be with us always, and Your promises to love us with an everlasting love. You came to give us an abundant life. We need to have our lives and our faith grounded in You. You provide the stability for our lives. You are our solid foundation, our rock, the source of our faith and love. We love You, dear God, and we need You. Thank you for listening to our prayers and for loving us with an everlasting love. Thank you for not delivering punishment but surrounding us with Your mercy and grace. Thank you for listening to our prayers and for providing for our needs. You are God, and we are Your humble servants. We ask these things in the name of Jesus. Amen.

Digging Deeper: What does God do to get your attention? What causes you to draw close to Him?

_____

_____

_____

_____

WORDS FOR
EVERYDAY LIVING

You are merciful and loving God. Your grace abounds, and You have blessed me beyond measure. You forgive me when I fail. I know that I have hurt others and have not loved them as You have loved me.

Although I may not acknowledge this often, I long for Your presence. My need for You is greater than my need for air to breathe and water to drink. These can only provide physical comfort and strength. You fill my soul and replenish my spiritual strength. You meet all my needs.

As the deer pants for water, so my soul longs for You. Fill the empty places of my heart with Your love. Renew my spirit and refresh my faith. Show me how to live for You.

My soul needs to be restored, refreshed, and encouraged. I need to be built up and prepared for action. Life in this world is a battle, and my strength needs to be renewed. My focus needs to be changed.

You gently guide and lead us. When we walk with You, everything falls into place, and there is great order amidst the chaos of this world. As we wander off on our own and try to do things our way, the perfect harmony is ruined, and the craziness of this world takes over.

You alone are worthy of our praise and adoration. You are worthy of our love and affection. You are to be glorified and honored above all. Your name should be worshiped and praised throughout the nations. One day every knee will bow and praise Your holy name.

As You have provided for Your people long ago, so You have provided for us each day. In the past, You brought Your people into the promised land and led them along the way. Today You have promised us heaven, a paradise for all eternity, our place to be with You forever.

We are but a small piece in this infinite puzzle. We are a small part of the eternal plan. We are very insignificant, but we know the One who knows all. We know the King of kings and the Lord of lords.

You, indeed, are our refuge and strength. You are our rock, our mighty fortress, our pillar of strength. If You are for us, who can be against us? If You are watching over us, we have nothing to fear. With Your support and encouragement, we can do all things.

Lord, You know what life is like in this world. Sometimes You would take a time out from the people, the pressures, the responsibilities, and You would spend time alone with Your Father. You needed time away to renew Your mind and restore Your strength and readjust Your focus. How much more do we need that special time?

We need You to reign in our hearts, in our lives, and in this world. We need You to be on the throne and in complete control. We need You to be the King of all the earth and the Lord of our lives.

You have restored our broken relationships and filled the void in our lives. You have given us meaning and purpose. You strengthen our faith and surround us with Your love.

You are truly awesome and incredible. You are our perfect example and our one true hope.

You have chosen to bless us with an abundance of love. Your Son piled the sins of the world on his back and carried the weight of our burdens to the cross. There is no greater example of love. Thank you for the unbelievable gifts of forgiveness, mercy, and compassion.

You came to give us love abundantly. We need to have our lives and our faith grounded in You. You provide the stability for our lives. You are our solid foundation, our rock, the source of our faith and love. We love You, dear God, and we need You.

SECTION 6:

Psalm 51-60

Day 119

Have mercy on me, O God, according to your unfailing love; according to your great compassion blot out my transgressions. Wash away all my iniquity and cleanse me from my sin. For I know my transgressions, and my sin is always before me.

Psalm 51:1-3

Dear Father in heaven,

You are mighty and all-powerful. You know all things. You know what we need before we even ask. You know the words on our lips before they are spoken. You know the deepest part of our hearts. You created us, and You know us better than we know ourselves. You can see the evil that is within our being. You can see the ugliness in our hearts. You see our sinful nature and our selfish desires. You know how often we fail and how far we have fallen away from You. Our sin creates a barrier, a huge wall that separates us from You. Sin destroys our relationship with You. Our sin turns our eyes away from You. Our focus is on ourselves. We need You, Father. We need to be cleansed and purified. We need to be washed and renewed. We need our sins to be taken away from us. We need forgiveness. We need to repent and turn away from the sins that so easily entangle us. We get caught up in the things, the desires, and all the distractions of this world. We get so busy and we fill our lives with different activities. We run from one place to another. We run and we race through life and sometimes we miss out on what is important. We don't take the time to listen to You. We don't stop to hear Your voice. You are crowded out by the craziness of our schedules and the demands on our time.

Dear God, please take away some of the busyness and chaos of this world. Clear our hearts and our minds of the clutter that is nonessential! Guard our hearts from the constant threats from the enemy. Help us to identify what is important and prioritize our lives. Teach us how to make time for You. Help us to seek You first. We have many transgressions, many sins, much evil and ugliness in our lives and in our hearts. We can't survive on our own in this world. We are persecuted. We are tempted. We are distracted. We are sinful. We are evil. Without You, there is no hope. Without You, we are lost in this world and throughout eternity. Have mercy upon us. Shower us with Your love and forgiveness. Wash away our sins, and fill us with Your abundant love and kindness. We need You today, tomorrow and forever. Thank you for answering our prayers and for never giving up on us. We ask all these things in the name of Jesus, our Savior and Lord. Amen.

Digging Deeper: What are the things of this world that waste your time and distract you from your relationship with God? How can you properly prioritize your time?

_____

_____

_____

_____

Day 120

Create in me a pure heart, O God, and renew a steadfast spirit within me. Do not cast me from your presence or take your Holy Spirit from me. Restore to me the joy of your salvation and grant me a willing spirit, to sustain me.

Psalm 51:10-12

Dear Lord,

David prayed this prayer to You when he needed forgiveness. He needed to be cleansed and purified by the Lord because he had been defiled. His heart was hardened and was wicked. He realized he had sinned.

Lord, I am a sinner also. I have sinned against You and against other people. I have not followed Your ways. I have been selfish. I do not seek to do the good deeds that You have called me to do, instead I do the evil and sinful things You have commanded me not to do. I do things that I hate. I am guilty. I deserve Your eternal punishment. I deserve to be condemned. I do not deserve Your mercy and Your grace. My sinful ways have separated me from You and caused me to fall away from You. Sometimes I get so caught up in the things of this world that I don't take time to walk with You or talk with You. I am wrapped up in my own little world. I need a Savior. I need to change my attitude and readjust my focus. I need to honestly examine my life and my heart. I need to look at my motives and my desires. I want to be more like You, Lord. I don't want to be selfish. I don't want to hurt the people that I love. I don't want to destroy my relationship with You and get tangled up in the cares and concerns of this world.

As David cried out to You for mercy and forgiveness, so I come humbly before You. I know that I have sinned and I am not worthy of You or a relationship with You. But You have paid the price for my sins. You have shown us the way of truth and You lead us in the way of salvation. You died so that I might live. You took my place. You came to this world to live a perfect life. Your mission was not complete until You died the perfect death. You, who knew no sin, took on the sins of the world. You took all my sin upon You and carried those sins to the cross. I have done nothing to earn my salvation. All has been a precious gift of love from You to me. Thank you for counting the cost and giving Your life for me. Thank you for Your unconditional love. Thank you for cleansing my heart and washing away my sins. Thank you for Your forgiveness. I humbly come before You in prayer in the name of Jesus, my Lord and Savior. Amen.

Digging Deeper: How are we like David? How do we open our hearts to accept the sustenance that God provides?

_____

_____

_____

_____

Day 121

But I am like an olive tree flourishing in the house of God; I trust in God's unfailing love for ever and ever. I will praise you forever for what you have done; in your name I will hope, for your name is good. I will praise you in the presence of your saints.

Psalm 52:8-9

Dear God,

I can do nothing on my own. Everything I have and everything I am are gifts from You. You have blessed me beyond measure. You are my Creator and my redeemer. You are the love of my life. I will praise Your holy name now and forevermore. You have restored my life and given me hope. You help to carry me through each day. Your guidance and strength are unlimited and truly necessary for my daily existence. I need You every minute of every day. When I try to do things on my own and desire to do things "my way," I fail miserably. With You, all things are possible. Without You, things go terribly wrong.

I am selfish and sinful. I want to be in control. I need to yield my heart and my life to Your perfect control and trust in Your perfect timing. When I step out on my own, relying on my own strength and ability, I am weak and fragile. I am easily distracted from the things that really matter. I am lost in the vastness of this world. I am wandering around without any true meaning or purpose. I need to be plugged into You and Your amazing power source. I need to seek You first. I need to allow You to work in and through my life. I need Your love. I need Your forgiveness. I need Your mercy and grace. Because of Your great love for me, I will praise You and give You thanks. I want to live my life in gratitude for all You have done for me. I want to shine Your light and share with others the great things that You have done in me and in my life. You are the one true God. You are incredibly strong and truly amazing. I am in awe of You, and I am surrounded by Your love. You are God, and yet You care about me. You are my Heavenly Father and You love me with an everlasting love. You are almighty and all-knowing, forgiving and merciful, holy and just. Thank you for caring about every aspect of my life. Thank you for supplying me with Your strength and mercy. Your forgiveness has changed my life and warmed my heart. Help me to lovingly share the gifts You have given me with others. I ask this all in Jesus' name. Amen.

Digging Deeper: How do we show praise on a daily basis for God's wonderful gifts? How do we continue to be grateful for everything He does for us? Why is this so important?

_____

_____

_____

_____

Day 122

The fool says in his heart, "There is no God." They are corrupt, and their ways are vile; there is no one who does good. God looks down from heaven on the sons of men to see if there are any who understand, any who seek God.

Psalm 53:1-2

Dear God,

Help me to always seek Your face and desire to spend time with You. Help me to want to be near You and to walk with You every day of my life. The fool says, "there is no God," but I know that You are real. I know that You are the one and only God, my Heavenly Father. It is difficult to understand exactly who You are. It is difficult to believe that the Creator of the world would care about me, one of the least of his creation. Yet Your love for me is powerful, it is life changing. Your love for me is so strong that it can move mountains and create faith. Your love for me is incomprehensible, because I am so undeserving. I have not followed You. I have not allowed You to have control of my heart and my life. I am still selfish. I am still caught up in the things of this world. I seek to fulfill my own desires instead of looking for ways to love and serve You. I am not perfect, and I will never be perfect. I am flawed. I am sinful. I need You! I need to have You working in my heart. I need to repent of my sins and have You cleanse my heart. I need You to replace the evil within me with Your goodness and mercy. I need to shower the people I love with Your perfect love. I need to share the blessings that I have received from You. You alone are God. I am Your humble servant. Give me the boldness and courage to share the faith that You have given me. Look down upon me with compassion and teach me how to love as You do. Help me to see others as Your precious children. Help me to share Your love with those around me. I need You! I know that other people need to know You as well. Let me be an instrument of Your love and peace. Help me to share Your tender mercies with those who need to know You. You are my precious Lord and Savior. Thank you for the many ways that You have saved me. Thank you for providing for all my needs. Thank you for the blessings You have given me every step of the way. In Your precious name, I lift up these requests. Amen.

Digging Deeper: What do you say to the person who claims, "There is no God"? How can you lovingly share your faith?

_____

_____

_____

_____

Day 123

Save me, O God, by your name; vindicate me by your might. Hear my prayer, O God; listen to the words of my mouth. Surely God is my help; the Lord is the one who sustains me.

Psalm 54:1-2, 4

Dear God, my Heavenly Father,

I know that You love me. I know that You care about every aspect of my life. I know that I am Your precious child. But sometimes I feel so alone. Sometimes, I feel lost. Sometimes I am unsure of which path to follow and where I should go. Lord, teach me Your ways and show me Your will for my life. Show me how I can love You and serve You with my whole heart. You are my strength and my shield. You are my rock and my fortress. You give me life and breath and You provide for my needs. My faith is renewed, and my heart is encouraged by spending time with You, by reading Your Word, and by pouring out my heart in prayer. Only You, dear God, truly know me. You know my wants and my needs. You know what is best for me. You know my strengths and weaknesses, all the positives and negatives in my life, the good and the evil. You are all-powerful, all-knowing, and almighty. You are God, the Creator of the entire universe, and You take the time to listen to my prayers.

Who am I that You should take notice of me? Who am I that You save me from my enemies? Who am I that You forgive me all of my sins? Who am I that You should care about me? My life is small and insignificant, but I am encouraged because You love me. You desire to have a relationship with me. I know that my parents love me, yet You love me perfectly and completely. I can do nothing to earn Your love or deserve Your mercy. You continue to fill my life and meet all my needs. Your kindness overflows in my life, and I have received blessing upon blessing. Your source of power and strength is limitless. You alone can do all things. You are in control of everything. Help me to yield to Your wisdom and to seek Your guidance. Thank you, dear God, for making my life complete and giving me a purpose for living. Thank you for loving me with an everlasting love. Thank you for answering my prayers and for showing me the way that I should live. I praise Your name and lift up all these requests in the name of Jesus. Amen.

Digging Deeper: Are there times when you are filled with doubt and have low self-esteem? Is it comforting to know that you are God's child and He created you as a special and unique person?

_____

_____

_____

_____

Day 124

Listen to my prayer, O God, do not ignore my plea; hear me and answer me. My thoughts trouble me and I am distraught at the voice of the enemy, at the stares of the wicked; for they bring down suffering upon me and revile me in their anger.

Psalm 55:1-3

Dearest God,

You are my Heavenly Father, and Your love for me is real. You want the absolute best for me. You have called me Your precious child. Please protect me from harm. Hold my hand and comfort me along life's path. Reveal to me Your perfect plan for my life. Show me the path that I should follow. Guide and lead me every day.

This world is filled with evil, and there is much suffering and pain. There are wicked people, and they want me to fail and to fall away from You. They persecute me day and night. They are angry and bitter. They do not know You and seem to have no interest in You. Help me to shine Your light and to share Your love with all people. Help me to encourage my family and friends and to lovingly share my faith even with my enemies. Give me boldness and courage. Help me not to be afraid, but to trust in You completely. When You are with me, I have nothing to fear. No one can separate me from You. Nothing can destroy my relationship with You. You give me hope and strength. You answer my cries for help. You listen to my prayers. You surround me with Your love.

Lord, sometimes it seems that the wicked prosper. The evil in this world is running rampant. People are persecuted for their faith. My enemies surround me. Life is sometimes so difficult. Show me how to keep my eyes focused on You. Help me not to be distracted and weighed down by the problems of this world. Let my heart not become discouraged. For You, dear Lord, can do all things and You are in complete control. You have overcome evil. You have defeated sin, death and Satan. You alone are God! Thank you for taking care of me and providing for my needs. Thank you for Your unconditional love and kindness. Thank you for Your presence in my life today and always. You have promised to never leave or forsake me. Thank you for touching my heart and changing my life. Thank you for allowing me to call You my Father and for loving me as Your child. In Your precious name, I pray. Amen.

Digging Deeper: How do you explain the prosperity of the wicked to non-believers? How can you show those around you that God is in complete control of everything in your life?

_____

_____

_____

_____

Day 125

My heart is in anguish within me; the terrors of death assail me. Fear and trembling have beset me; horror has overwhelmed me. I said, "Oh, that I had the wings of a dove! I would fly away and be at rest—I would flee far away and stay in the desert; I would hurry to my place of shelter, far from the tempest and the storm."

Psalm 55:4-8

Dear God,

The weight of the world is on my shoulders. I am overwhelmed by the troubles and trials that I am facing. I am afraid of what the future holds. I am not sure I have the strength to face each new day. I am filled with fear, and my heart is heavy. I know that I cannot make it on my own. I am weak and my faith sometimes wavers. There are so many difficulties to face. I am tired, I am troubled, I am fearful, and I am weak. I can't make it on my own. I feel alone and I am discouraged.

I need You every minute of every day. I need Your strength and Your courage. I need to feel Your loving arms around me. I know that You are all-powerful. When I am weak, You remain strong. When I am lost and alone, I need to believe that You are always with me. When I am overwhelmed, I believe that You are ready, willing and able to carry my burdens. You listen to me when I call. You answer when I cry out. You comfort me when I am afraid, and

You provide when I am lacking. You are the shelter I seek when my life is filled with storms. You are my fortress, and You always keep me safe. When I need rest, You restore my soul. You fill my life with peace and take away my fear. You wipe the tears from my eyes and take care of my every need. Someday my life will return to normal, and I will be carefree. I will not be weighed down; I will be free and unburdened. But I know that at all times and in all places, You are with me. I am never truly alone. You are my strength and my shield. You are my solid rock and the cornerstone of my faith. I can put my hope and my trust in You. You honor the promises that You have given us in Your holy Word, the Bible. Thank you for the many blessings You have given to me, especially for Your love. I give You all my troubles, trials, problems, and burdens and pray that You will carry me through. I lift up all these requests in the name of Jesus, my Savior and Lord. Amen.

Digging Deeper: Have you ever wanted to run away from your problems? Where would you go and what would you do? Does God have a better answer for you?

_____

_____

_____

_____

Day 126

Cast your cares on the Lord and he will sustain you; he will never let the righteous fall. But you, O God, will bring down the wicked into the pit of corruption; bloodthirsty and deceitful men will not live out half their days. But as for me, I trust in you.

Psalm 55:22-23

Dear Lord,

I confess that I like to be in control. I want to be strong and to take care of myself. Sometimes I am filled with pride and my sinfulness draws me away from You. But I know in my heart that I need You. I am truly weak, and You have an unlimited source of knowledge and strength. Your ways are far above my ways, and Your thoughts are infinitely greater than my thoughts. Why do I think that I can handle all the problems, troubles, and trials of this life on my own? Why do I think that my way is best? Why am I unwilling to let You work in my life and soften my heart? Sometimes I am stubborn. Sometimes I am narrow-minded. Sometimes I am hard-hearted. Lord, I need You to show me the way, the truth, and the life that I should be living. I need to cast all my cares upon You, Lord, and allow You to carry my burdens. I try to do things myself, and that is when I fail. I try to handle everything on my own, and the problems overwhelm me, and I am discouraged. I can't do every-thing perfectly, and I fall short of my standard and of Your perfect standard. I need a Savior! I need someone to pull me out of the pit and get me back on track. I need someone who is stronger, smarter, wiser, more powerful, loving, and discerning to help me when I am lost. I need someone who will not let me down. I need someone that I can trust completely. I need You, Lord.

Evil men desire to hurt me, to corrupt me, to bring me down, and to destroy me. Every day I face new challenges and new problems. But You have promised to be with me through it all. You have promised to carry me when I can no longer walk on my own. You will give me Your wisdom and strength. You will give me peace in the midst of trouble. You will wipe my tears and give me joy in the journey. You will replace my doubt with faith. You will surround me with love that is greater than all my fears.

When I am afraid, I will trust in You. When I am lost, help me to seek Your face and Your guidance. When I am burdened, please help carry my load. Strip me of my pride and the sin that destroys my relationship with You. And Lord, please forgive me and help me to be the person that You created me to be. I ask this in the name of Jesus. Amen.

Digging Deeper: Do you "cast your cares on the Lord"? How do you know that He will sustain you?

_____

_____

_____

_____

Day 127

When I am afraid, I will trust in you. In God, whose word
I praise, in God I trust; I will not be afraid. What can mortal man do to me? All day long they twist my words; they
are always plotting to harm me. They conspire, they lurk,
they watch my steps, eager to take my life.

Psalm 56:3-6

Dear God,

I do trust in You completely. You are worthy of all honor and
praise. You are in control of my every step. My foot does not hit the
ground without Your knowledge. You know when I stand and when
I lie down. You know where I am going and where I have been. You
know my friends and my enemies. You know everything there is to
know about me. You are my Creator, my father, my provider, my
rock, my fortress, my shelter, my comforter, and my redeemer. You
are an amazing, wonderful, loving, and caring God!

I know that You will take care of me. I know that there is nothing
in this world that can separate me from Your love. Mortal man cannot destroy my relationship with You. My enemies may be able to
hurt me physically, but You are always with me. Although they desire
to see me fall, You want to rescue me. You will go into the depths
of the earth to pull me out, pick me up and carry me. Although evil
men plot to harm me, You give me strength and courage. You guide
and lead me in the path I should follow. You are my God! You have

overcome evil with good. You have listened to my cries for help. You have answered my prayers. You have blessed me every day of my life. All I have comes from You. You are worthy of my trust and my love. I do not need to be afraid because I have You in my life. You give me strength for the day and for every trial and trouble that I encounter. You have not promised that my life would be easy, but You have promised to be with me. I know that I am Your child and Your love for me is real. Help me not to doubt. Help me not to be afraid. Help me to trust in what is real and to know that You are God and You are in control of every situation. I pray all these things in the name of Jesus, my Savior and Lord. Amen.

Digging Deeper: What can mortal man do to you? If God is for you, who can be against you?

Day 128

Have mercy on me, O God, have mercy on me, for in you my soul takes refuge. I will take refuge in the shadow of your wings until the disaster has passed. I cry out to God Most High, to God who fulfills his purpose for me. He sends from heaven and saves me, rebuking those who hotly pursue me; God sends his love and his faithfulness.

Psalm 57:1-3

Dear God,

Have mercy on me. Show me Your grace and fill my life with Your love. Give me shelter from the storms of life and give me strength to face each new day. I know that I am a sinner. I do not deserve Your love and kindness. I deserve to be punished. I deserve to be abandoned. On my own, I do not have any hope. I am weak and weary. My soul is burdened and my life is bleak. But You have rescued me. You give my life meaning and purpose. You forgive my sinful ways, and You have changed my heart. You have blessed me time and time again. I am unworthy of Your mercy and grace, but I am so thankful for Your abundant gifts.

Sometimes I am overwhelmed, but I know that You are with me always. You will never desert me or fail me. You are faithful even when I am not. You are always waiting for me with open arms. Sometimes I wander away and get lost in the problems of this world. You don't condemn me or withhold Your love for me. I am like the prodigal son who gets tangled up in the ways of the world and leaves his father. But You are God, our heavenly Father, and You always warmly welcome me into Your house, into Your fold, and into Your arms. When I am lost, sometimes You even come and search for me. When I am frightened, You wrap Your loving arms around me and keep me safe. When I am without hope, You show me the plans that You have for me and my life.

Lord, help me to trust in You completely. Help me not to wander off and get distracted from all the things that really matter. Help me to seek You first in my life, for I know that You will always take good care of me. Restore my soul and my strength. Watch over me and keep me safe. Protect me from my enemies and those who desire to see me fail. Help me to weather each storm. Thank you for Your mercy and grace. Thank you for listening to my prayers. In Your precious name, I pray. Amen.

Digging Deeper: What are the things in your life that remind you of the hope that God provides? How do you continue to trust God despite the problems of the world?

_____

_____

_____

_____

Day 129

My heart is steadfast, O God, my heart is steadfast; I will sing and make music. I will praise you, O Lord, among the nations; I will sing of you among the peoples. For great is your love, reaching to the heavens; your faithfulness reaches to the skies. Be exalted, O God, above the heavens; let your glory be over all the earth.

Psalm 57:7, 9-11

Dear God,

You are worthy of praise. You are worthy of glory. You are worthy of honor. You are worthy of our complete love and trust. You are worthy of our trust and our devotion. You alone are worthy. I want to sing Your praises. I want to yell it from that mountain tops that You are God. You created each one of us. You redeemed us. You forgive us. You surround us with Your mercy. You give us abundant blessings, and Your grace overflows into our hearts and our lives. We cannot truly live without You. You have given us a precious treasure, the opportunity to know You and to love You. You have filled our cups with blessings and our lives with love.

You are an awesome and amazing God, and yet You care about each one of us. You care about every detail of our lives. You patiently listen to our prayers. You lovingly answer our requests. We commit every detail of our lives to You, and yet You already know everything there is to know about us. You are in complete control of the entire world. We humbly come before You, bow down, worship, and adore You. We are not worthy of coming into Your presence. You have created a way for us to have fellowship with You. You sent Your one and only Son, Jesus into this world. He came to repair the damage in our lives and in our world because of sin. Sin separates us from You. Sin takes our eyes off of You. Pride destroys our relationships with others and our relationship with You. Soften our hearts, Lord. Take away our sinful desires and evil within our hearts. Create in us a clean heart. Break down the walls of sin and renew our relationships. Forgive us and help us to forgive others. Teach us how to walk with You and live the life that You have created for us. Help us to yield to Your will and desire to walk in Your ways all the days of our lives. Thank you for Your faithfulness. Help us to sing Your praises and tell others of Your love. We pray that Your love and Your light would shine through our lives and others would be drawn to You. In the name of Jesus, Your Son and our Lord, we pray. Amen.

Digging Deeper: How does pride destroy your relationship with God and with others? When has pride caused problems in your life?

Day 130

Do you rulers indeed speak justly? Do you judge uprightly among men? No, in your heart you devise injustice; and your hands mete out violence on the earth. Then men will say, "Surely the righteous still are rewarded; surely there is a God who judges the earth."

Psalm 58:1-2, 11

Dear God,

Only You are a righteous judge. Only You are above reproach. Only You are holy and just. Lord, the rulers of this world are not perfect. They are sometimes corrupt. They do not seek to follow Your ways or follow Your will. They enjoy the power that they have, and they want to control all things. Their ways are not Your ways, and their ideas are based on human wisdom and not godly knowledge.

Lord, we live in a fallen world. There is evil all around us. People are selfish and self-centered. They want what they want, when they want it! They do not care about whom they hurt or how they hurt them. The world says that every one should look out for themselves. People should take care of number one!

But, Lord, You care about us. Your love for us is real. Your concern for our lives and our relationships is genuine. You are righteous and just. You are perfect and holy. You have given us the Bible to guide and lead us and have sent Your Holy Spirit to show us the way. We should seek You first and seek to do Your will for our lives.

You have lovingly spoken the truth to us in Your Word. You have given us guidelines to live by and commands to follow. You discipline us as a loving Heavenly Father. You forgive us over and over again. You have poured out blessings upon our lives. Your mercy and grace overflow in our lives. We deserve so little, and yet You have given us so much! You are the great provider. You are a righteous judge. You will judge this world and punish the evil and bless Your children. Those who have chosen to ignore You in this world will be cast away from You for all eternity. Those who love You and cling to Your cross and Your salvation will be with You forever. You are an amazing God. Thank you for loving us and listening to our prayers. Thank you for Your forgiveness, Your mercy, and Your grace. Thank you for Your love. In the name of Jesus, our Savior and Lord, we pray. Amen.

Digging Deeper: The leaders and rulers of this world are human; only God is righteous, holy, and just. How does their justice compare with God's? Why must God judge the world?

_____

_____

_____

_____

Day 131

Deliver me from my enemies, O God; protect me from those who rise up against me. Deliver me from evildoers and save me from bloodthirsty men. But I will sing of your strength, in the morning I will sing of your love; for you are my fortress, my refuge in times of trouble.

Psalm 59:1-2, 16-17

Dear God,

Only You can protect me. Only You can watch over me. Only You can keep me safe today and always. My enemies are all around me. Sometimes they are people I know; sometimes they are people I don't know. Sometimes my enemies are the things that rob me of my time and talents, things that take me away from You, my Savior and Lord. Sometimes my enemies are the worries that plague me or the problems that overwhelm me. Sometimes my enemies are the temptations that surround me or the evil that is within me. I am weak. I try to do things on my own and my strength isn't sufficient. I need You, dear God. I need Your unlimited source of wisdom and strength. I need to seek refuge within Your arms. I need Your guidance. I need You every day. I need Your love. I need to spend time with You. I need Your forgiveness. I need to hear Your Word and to be encouraged by You. You know what I need. You know my strengths and weaknesses. You know my joys and sorrows. You know my wants and needs. You know my heart and my desires. Help me to desire to live my life in accordance with Your will. Help me to look to You to meet my needs and not cling to the things of this world. My priorities get confused, and I get caught up in the ways of this world.

I know that You are my everlasting source of strength and love. You are my refuge, my fortress, my rock, my shield, my hope, and my joy. You alone give me the peace that passes all understanding, and You fill my life with meaning. Help me to sing Your praises and glorify and honor You with my life. Take away the evil, the sinfulness, the problems, and troubles that plague me. Gently guide me with Your loving arms and show me Your perfect path. Help me to be the person that You created me to be. Shine Your light and Your love into my life and help me to be a good ambassador for You. I ask all these things in the name of the One who came to give me life, Jesus, who is my Savior and Lord. Amen.

Digging Deeper: What does it mean to you to have God as your refuge and your fortress? Describe a specific time when God delivered you or protected you from your enemies.

_____

_____

_____

_____

Day 132

You have rejected us, O God, and burst forth upon us; you have been angry—now restore us! You have shaken the land and torn it open; mend its fractures, for it is quaking. Save us and help us with your right hand that those you love may be delivered.

Psalm 60:1-2, 5

Dear God,

You must be so disappointed in us. You created us, and You have given us everything that we need. You want to pour out Your blessings upon our lives. But we have rejected You. We have turned away from You. We have chosen to follow our own hearts. We have chosen to do things our own way. You must be hurt as You look out over Your incredible creation and see so many people who are truly lost. Some people are hostile toward You, and some people don't even care about You or acknowledge You. We are hard-hearted, and we are rebellious. We are filled with pride. We are sinful. We are evil. Sometimes we are totally out of control. You stand by longing to reach out to help us and we continually ignore You. We don't accept Your help or Your blessings. We prefer to fail on our own than to ask You for anything. We are a stubborn people. We are blinded by our sins and oblivious to our true needs. We seek to fill our lives with things that have little true value or importance. We are chasing after the wrong goals. We are seeking joy and acceptance in the wrong places. We want what we can't have, and we are drawn away from You by the many distractions in this world.

You have created this world and it is Yours to do with what You please. When we have turned away from You, You must be angry with us. When we reject Your ways, Your heart must break. When we continue in our sinful ways and do not seek You, You must long to help us. Do not punish us in Your anger or reject us forever. Pour out Your love and forgiveness into our lives. Save us from ourselves and our wickedness and pride. Deliver us from evil. Show us Your will for our lives. Help us to break free from the bondage of sin. Tear down the walls of pride that separate us from You. Restore our relationship with You. Forgive us for rejecting You and turning away from You. Create in us a new heart and draw near to us. Thank you that Your love overcomes evil and You have defeated sin, death, and the devil. Fill us with Your power. We ask all this in the name of Jesus. Amen.

Digging Deeper: When you see those around you struggling with evil and sin in their life, how do you show them the value of finding God's plans?

_____

_____

_____

_____

WORDS FOR EVERYDAY LIVING

Dear God, please take away some of the busyness and chaos of this world. Clear our hearts and our minds of the clutter that is nonessential! Guard our hearts from the constant threats from the enemy. Help us to identify what is important and prioritize our lives.

I need to change my attitude and readjust my focus. I need to honestly examine my life and my heart. I need to look at my motives and my desires. I want to be more like You, Lord.

Thank you for supplying me with Your strength and mercy. Your forgiveness has changed my life and warmed my heart. Help me to lovingly share the gifts You have given me with others.

Help me to always seek Your face and desire to spend time with You. Help me to want to be near You and to walk with You every day of my life. The fool says there is no God, but I know that You are real. I know that You are the one and only God, my Heavenly Father.

Who am I that You should take notice of me? Who am I that You save me from my enemies? Who am I that You forgive me all of my sins? Who am I that You should care about me?

Show me how to keep my eyes focused on You. Help me not to be distracted and weighed down by the problems of this world. Let my heart not become discouraged. For You, dear Lord, can do all things, and You are in complete control.

You are the shelter I seek when my life is filled with storms. You are my fortress, and You always keep me safe. When I need rest, You restore my soul. You fill my life with peace and take away my fear.

You will give me Your wisdom and strength. You will give me peace in the midst of trouble. You will wipe my tears and give me joy in the journey. You will replace my doubt with faith. You will surround me with love that is greater than all my fears.

You have not promised that my life would be easy, but You have promised to be with me. I know that I am Your child, and Your love for me is real. Help me not to doubt. Help me not to be afraid. Help me to trust in what is real and to know that You are God and You are in control of every situation.

I am like the prodigal son who gets tangled up in the ways of the world and leaves his father. But You are God, our heavenly Father, and You always warmly welcome me into Your house, into Your fold, and into Your arms.

You have given us a precious treasure, the opportunity to know You and to love You. You have filled our cups with blessings and our lives with love.

You discipline us as a loving Heavenly Father. You forgive us over and over again. You have poured out blessings upon our lives. Your mercy and grace overflow in our lives. We deserve so little, and yet You have given us so much!

My enemies are all around me. Sometimes they are people I know; sometimes they are people I don't know. Sometimes my enemies are the things that rob me of my time and talents, things that take me away from You, my Savior and Lord. Sometimes my enemies are the worries that plague me or the problems that overwhelm me.

We are a stubborn people. We are blinded by our sins and oblivious to our true needs. We seek to fill our lives with things that have little true value or importance. We are chasing after the wrong goals. We are seeking joy and acceptance in the wrong places.

SECTION 7:

Psalm 61-70

Day 133

Hear my cry, O God; listen to my prayer. From the ends of the earth I call to you, I call as my heart grows faint; lead me to the rock that is higher than I. For you have been my refuge, a strong tower against the foe. I long to dwell in your tent forever and take refuge in the shelter of your wings.

Psalm 61:1-4

O Dear God,

My heart grows weary and I have no strength. Trouble surrounds me. My enemies are winning the battle. I cry out and no one hears me. I feel so alone. I don't know which way to go and what direction to turn. I cannot see over the rising floods. I will not survive on my own.

Lord, I ask You once again, come and help me. Save me from my enemies. Restore my strength and my soul. I am weak. I am lost. I need You. You alone can save me. Wrap me in Your loving arms. Shelter me from the storms of life. You are my refuge. Lift me out of the pit. Show me the way, Your perfect way that I might follow. Lead me beside the still waters, and quiet the winds and the waves that threaten me.

God, You are almighty. You can do all things. You have promised to provide for my needs. You listen to my prayers, and You answer them. You have promised never to leave me. When the cares and concerns of this world are too much for me, You are with me. When my troubles cloud my way, You will guide me. When I am lost and alone, You will comfort me. When the floodwaters are rising, You will be my shelter. When I cannot continue on my own, You will carry me. When I have made a mess of my life, You forgive me and surround me with Your love. Your love for me is immeasurable. Your power supply is endless. Your willingness to provide for me exceeds my ability to even ask. You know what I need before the words reach my mouth. You know my thoughts before they are spoken. You know my heart and my motives, and yet You still love me. Help me to be more like You. Create in me a new heart and take away the sinful desires and the evil that is within me. Help me to become the person that You created me to be. Thank you for the privilege of spending time with You and the ability to go to Your House. Thank you for Your Word that blesses my soul and for Your Spirit that guides and leads me. Thank you for always listening to the cry of my heart. I humbly come before You in prayer lifting up these requests in the name of Jesus, my Savior. Amen.

Digging Deeper: How much time do you spend in prayer each day? Do you have a specific time of day when you pray? Do you pray in a special place? Or is your prayer time a running dialogue with God throughout the day?

_____

_____

_____

_____

Day 134

Find rest, O my soul, in God alone; my hope comes from him. He alone is my rock and my salvation; he is my fortress, I will not be shaken. My salvation and my honor depend on God; he is my mighty rock, my refuge. Trust in him at all times, O people; pour out your hearts to him, for God is our refuge.

Psalm 62:5-8

Dearest Heavenly Father,

My hope truly comes from You. Your love for me is incredible, and Your grace is sufficient for me. You give rest to my soul and provide comfort and strength to face each new day. I know that whatever comes before me today, You will be with me. You will carry me through. If I can't make it on my own, You will take care of me. You are perfect and Your will is perfect. You will not let me face any problem that is too great for me to bear. You have promised to always be with me; not just during the good times but during the bad times. You will never leave me or forsake me. You will be my rock and my fortress. There is nothing that can separate me from Your love. You will hold me in Your arms and be my guide. In You, all things are possible. With You, I can face the trials and temptations of each day. You give us our daily bread which means that all I need I will receive from You.

Thank you for listening to my prayers and listening to the deep needs of my soul. Sometimes I can't form the words to say. Sometimes I can't speak the words, but You know my heart and You know my needs. You want to provide for me and share Your abundant blessings with me. I have done nothing to earn or deserve Your love. You give it to me unconditionally and with no strings attached. Your love fulfills my soul and fills all the emptiness in my life. You give without ceasing and love without limits. You are the perfect example for us. Help me to be more like You. Teach me Your will for my life. Let Your love shine though me so that others may be drawn to You. Be my light and my guide through this crazy, busy, stress-filled, yet wonderful world. Help me to keep my eyes focused on You and to trust in You completely. Help my unbelief and restore my faith. Answer the questions that are in my heart, and draw me close to You. You alone are God. Thank you for touching my heart and changing my life forever. I humbly come before You and lift up my requests in the name of Jesus, Your Son and my Savior. Amen.

Digging Deeper: We live in a busy, chaotic world. Where does your soul find rest? Do you take time to renew your faith, to restore your strength, and to find God's peace?

_____

_____

_____

_____

Day 135

> O God, you are my God, earnestly I seek you ; my soul thirsts for you, my body longs for you, in a dry and weary land where there is no water. I have seen you in the sanctuary and beheld your power and your glory. I will praise you as long as I live, and in your name I will lift up my hands.
>
> Psalm 63:1-2, 4

Dear God,

When I seek You, I always find You. When I call, You listen to my cry. When I pray, You answer my prayers. There is no one like You. You are holy and just, righteous and perfect in every way. You have made me a unique and wonderful person. There is no one in this world exactly like me. You have called me to be Your child and given me the opportunity to have a relationship with You. I am the clay, and You are the potter. You shaped me and formed me, and You continue to work in and through my life. You provide me with all that I need in this world. When I am hungry, You give me physical food and spiritual nourishment though Your holy Word. When I am thirsty, You give me water to drink, and You quench the deep thirst of my soul to be in Your presence. When I am weary and wandering aimlessly through life, You direct my paths and renew my strength.

When I look at the heavens, I am filled with awe and wonder. Your creation is beautiful and inspiring beyond words. When I look at the mountains and their grandeur, I am amazed at how majestic this world is. When I look at the oceans and watch the waves crashing to the shore, I see how small I am and how incredible is Your world. Yet, You take the time to listen to me. You have touched my soul. I want to sing Your praises and tell the world of Your power and might. I want to praise Your name and share Your love with those around me. Give me boldness and courage. Help me not to be ashamed of You or my relationship with You. Help me to live the life that You created for me. Help me to trust in You completely. Help me to find the beauty in this world and focus on the blessings that You have given to me. Help me to be thankful for who I am and for You, my maker, my Creator and my Heavenly Father. Thank you for always listening to me and answering my prayers. Thank you for Your provisions and Your grace. Thank you for Your forgiveness and Your strength. I pray all this in Your precious name. Amen.

Digging Deeper: Do you earnestly seek God? Do you thirst for God? Do you long to spend time with Him? Or do you take your relationship with God for granted?

_____

_____

_____

_____

Day 136

Hear me, O God, as I voice my complaint; protect my life from the threat of the enemy. Hide me from the conspiracy of the wicked, from that noisy crowd of evildoers. They sharpen their tongues like swords and aim their words like deadly arrows. Let the righteous rejoice in the Lord and take refuge in him; let all the upright in heart praise him!

Psalm 64:1-3, 10

Dear God,

Sometimes it seems like the whole world is out to get me. I have so many enemies. There are so many people who want to see me fail. They persecute me. They mock me. They insult me. They hurt me. I feel lost and alone. I am threatened and I am afraid. But I know that You can hear my voice. You hear my cries in the night. You listen to my prayers. You love me, and I know that You are with me always. I am never truly alone because You have promised to never leave me. Although my enemies conspire against me and look for ways to bring me down, You are always there to build me up and encourage me. In You, I can do all things. In You, I have power and strength and courage. In You, I have hope. Your love drives out all fear. You sustain me, and You provide for my needs. When the weight of the world is on my shoulders, You will carry my burden and me.

Help me to praise You at all times. Help me to acknowledge You when things are going well and give You the glory, honor, and praise.

Help me to seek You when times are tough and look to You for courage and strength. Let me sing Your praises and worship You every day of my life. Let me rejoice in You, Lord, and let my heart sing. For You alone should be worshiped and praised. You are worthy! You are almighty! You alone are God! Protect me from all evil and harm. Restore my faith and my strength when I am weary. Forgive me when I waiver and doubt. Renew my spirit. Let Your light and Your love shine through me. Help me to have victory over my enemies for Your name sake. Let me praise You with my life now and forevermore. Thank you for the many blessings You have given to me. Help me to live my life in a manner that is pleasing to You. In Jesus' name who lived and died for me and who suffered so that I might live. Amen.

Digging Deeper: How can you praise God with your life? What does it mean to live a life worthy of your calling?

_____

_____

_____

_____

Day 137

Praise awaits you, O God, in Zion; to you our vows will be fulfilled. O you who hear prayer, to you all men will come. When we were overwhelmed by sins, you atoned for our transgressions. Blessed is the man you choose and bring near to live in your courts! We are filled with the good things of your house, of your holy temple.

Psalm 65:1-4

Dear God,

We are blessed because we know You and we can call You our Father. You have chosen us to be Your children, and You have restored our relationship with You. You have given us blessing upon blessing and filled our lives with great and glorious gifts. We are blessed because of Your grace and Your incomparable love and kindness. We can come to You because You have called us.

We are sinful. We are undeserving. We are not worthy to be called Your children. We fail, and we fall down. We disappoint You, and we hurt those around us. We are not perfect as You are. Our hearts and our desires are evil. We are selfish, and we are self-centered. We need forgiveness. Our hearts and our lives need to be cleansed. We need You because we can't make it on our own. We try our best, but it isn't good enough. Our motives aren't pure. Our actions are not holy. We deceive others, and we even deceive ourselves. We want to be the people that You have created us to be, but we do not have the strength to do it on our own. We need Your strength. We need Your love. We need You in every aspect of our lives. Thank you for paying the price for our sinful ways and for dying on the cross for us.

We come before You humbled. We beg Your forgiveness and pray that You would work in our lives. Help us to be more like You and to desire the things that You desire. Help us to seek You first and to seek Your will for our lives. Help us to be thankful and to live our lives to give You the glory, honor, and praise. We need more of You and less of ourselves. Create in us a clean heart. We ask these things in the name of Jesus, our Lord and Savior. Amen.

Digging Deeper: What are the benefits of humility? How does humility make it easier for us to feel God's presence in our daily lives?

_____

_____

_____

_____

Day 138

You answer us with awesome deeds of righteousness, O God our Savior, the hope of all the ends of the earth and the farthest seas, who formed the mountains by your power, having armed yourself with strength, who stilled the roaring of the seas, the roaring of their waves, and the turmoil of the nations. Those living far away fear your wonders; where morning dawns and evening fades you call forth songs of joy.

Psalm 65:5-8

Dear God our Savior,

Our hope is in You alone. Although the waves rise up against us, You can control the roaring seas. Although the storms of this world threaten to overtake us, You can calm the winds and the waves. Although the turmoil and craziness of this world can burden our hearts and our souls, You have overcome the world. You are almighty. You are awesome. You can do all things. We are in awe of Your mighty works and Your deeds of righteousness. You have created this entire world. You formed the mountains. You made the oceans. You filled the sky with birds and the lands with animals. You made the flowers and the trees. You spoke the whole world into existence. We are humbled in Your presence. We bow down and worship You. We are amazed at Your creative powers. Your creative powers are displayed throughout the universe. As each day begins, the sun You made rises and many days end with the incredible masterpiece of colors parading across the skies at sunset. All these things are the works of Your fingers. Each person is a unique child of Yours whether they are willing to believe that fact or not.

You are the one and only God and You allow us, Your creation, to come before You in prayer. You listen to us and You love us. You calm the storms of our lives and clean up the mess we make of our world. You are in complete control. You were there in the beginning of the world, and You will be there in the end. You are the Alpha and the Omega. You are to be worshiped and praised now and forevermore. Thank you for creating us and for changing our lives with Your love. Thank you for listening to our prayers and for teaching us how to love. Forgive us for the chaos that we create and give us Your perfect peace. We pray this in the name of Jesus, our Savior and Lord. Amen.

Digging Deeper: What problems, troubles, trials and/or chaos burden your heart and soul? How can you give these over to God? Do you believe that He can quiet the storms that reign in your life?

_____

_____

_____

_____

Day 139

Shout with joy to God, all the earth! Sing the glory of his name; offer him glory and praise! Say to God, "How awesome are your deeds! So great is your power that your enemies cringe before you. All the earth bows down to you; they sing praise to you, they sing praise to your name."

Psalm 66:1-4

Dear God,

In Your Word it says to "shout with joy" to You. Most of the time, we are afraid to even talk to You. We come humbly before You. We whisper our prayers—if we verbalize them at all. You are encouraging us to shout to You and to sing Your praise and to offer You the glory, honor, and praise that You deserve. We need to boldly worship You and to raise our voices to glorify Your name. You are almighty. You are worthy of praise. We should be shouting Your name from the rooftops and the mountaintops! You are our Heavenly Father. You created us and redeemed us. You have changed our lives and given us life. You fill us with great joy! Your love is amazing and truly incredible. We need to share the precious gifts that You have given to us. We need to sing Your praises and openly worship You. You have given us every good and perfect gift! You deserve all praise, not just from our lips and our voices, but from our hearts!

We are Your witnesses. We are Your ambassadors. Help us to shine Your light and share Your love with others. You alone are God!

We are merely Your servants, and we have been called to be Your children. You have chosen us, and we are truly blessed! Help us not to be ashamed of our faith but to lovingly share what we believe with those around us. As we think about how awesome You are and how wonderful and powerful You are, give us the courage to talk with others about You. And help us to always sing joyfully and to lovingly share our faith with our lips, our voices, our hearts and our lives. Blessed are we because You have chosen us…help us to share our blessings with others through our words, our deeds, our actions, and our lives. In the name of Jesus, our Lord and Savior, we pray. Amen.

Digging Deeper: Think of a time when you were filled with great joy. With whom did you want to share your wonderful news? With whom do you want to share the good news of the gospel? Do you regularly pray for these people?

_____

_____

_____

_____

Day 140

> Come and see what God has done, how awesome his works in man's behalf! He turned the sea into dry land, they passed through the water on foot—come, let us rejoice in him. He rules forever by his power, his eyes watch the nations—let not the rebellious rise up against him.
>
> Psalm 66:5-7

Dear God,

You are a gracious and loving God. You desire to watch over us and take care of us. You listen to our prayers and You answer them. You created the entire world, and You can do all things. Throughout the Bible, Your great and awesome works are chronicled. When Moses was leading Your people out of slavery and out of Egypt, You turned the sea into dry land. You provided a way when there seemed to be no solution. You always provide a way for us. When we are lost, You guide and lead us. When we are discouraged, You are there to comfort us. When we are overwhelmed, You find a way to meet our needs. When we are burdened, You are there to carry our load. When we are guilty, You offer forgiveness. When we are lonely, You lovingly wrap Your arms around us and remind us that we are special to You and we are Your children. When we feel worthless, You remind us that we were chosen and called by You and we are precious in Your sight. When we feel defeated by our enemies, You whisper to us that You have defeated all our enemies and You are in control.

The things of this world will all pass away, but our Heavenly Father is the Alpha and the Omega, the beginning and the end. He was, and is, and evermore shall be the one and only God. He is amazing and His love for us is never-failing and eternal. God, You have given us all things and You continue to provide for our every need. When it seems that there is no way for us to go, You create a way, You provide a miracle, You show us Your way. You are "the Way, the Truth and the Life." (John 14:6) We are blessed to know You and privileged to call You "our Father." You are holy and just, loving and compassionate, caring and giving. You are perfect and we are so undeserving of Your grace and mercy. Thank you for Your abundant provisions and Your incredible blessings. Help us to proclaim Your tender mercies to those around us and show others the forgiveness that You have shown us. In the name of Jesus, our Savior, we pray. Amen.

Digging Deeper: What has the Lord been doing in your life? What is He teaching you? How is the Holy Spirit leading you?

_____

_____

_____

_____

Day 141

Come and listen, all you who fear God; let me tell you what he has done for me. I cried out to him with my mouth; his praise was on my tongue…but God has surely listened and heard my voice in prayer. Praise be to God, who has not rejected my prayer or withheld his love from me.

Psalm 66:16-17, 19-20

Dear God,

I have cried out to You. Sometimes, I can hardly utter the words. I am overwhelmed by the trials and problems that I encounter. I am exhausted by the expectations and the responsibilities that I have. I can hardly tread water; I feel as if I am going to drown. I am sinking, I am falling, and I can barely survive! But You, O God, are mighty and powerful. You are faithful and just. You are caring and giving. You can pull me out of the pit that has entrapped me. You can pick me up when I have fallen. You can restore my strength and my health. You can lift the burdens from my back and carry my load for me. Although I have failed, You never will. Although I am weak, You are strong. Although I have sinned, You are holy. Although I am lost, You have sent Your Spirit to guide me along the path and show me the way.

Thank you for never giving up on me. Although I have doubts, You are always faithful. Although I deserve punishment, You give me mercy and love. Although I have turned away from You and have followed my own desires, You forgive me and gently lead me back into Your loving arms. Let me praise You with my whole heart and with my life. Let me sing Your praises and encourage others to seek You. Let me share Your love with those around me. Let me worship You and praise You for the many wonderful things that You have done for me. You have always been faithful even when I am not! Your love for me is never-ending. I can do nothing to earn Your love; it is a precious gift bestowed upon me. I am sinful and time after time, You forgive me. I pray that Your love would flow through me. Teach me Your ways and show me the path that I should follow. Help me to seek You first and to live my life in a manner that is pleasing to You. In Jesus' name I pray. Amen.

Digging Deeper: What are some of the prayers that God has answered in your life? How do you respond to Him after your prayers are answered? Do you thank Him and give Him the glory, honor, and praise?

_____

_____

_____

_____

Day 142

May God be gracious to us and bless us and make his face shine upon us; may your ways be known on earth; your salvation among all nations. May the peoples praise you, O God; may all the peoples praise you.

Psalm 67:1-3

Dear God,

We pray for Your blessings and Your tender mercies to be bestowed upon us. Be gracious unto us and fill our lives with Your blessings. Smile upon us and show us Your love and kindness. Fill our lives with meaning, and be a real part of each of our days. Show us Your Word, Your will and plan for our lives. Make known to us the path that we should follow. Give us the strength and courage to walk in Your ways. Help us to keep our eyes focused on You. Help us not to become entangled in the sinful ways of this world. Help us not to worry about the trivial and insignificant details of our lives. Help us to focus on the things with an eternal value. Let us look to You and Your Word to help us to encourage Your people.

Lord, we want to see Your name worshiped and glorified. You are truly worthy of our praise. Help us to shine the light of Your love with those around us. Lord, we are afraid to share our love for You with others. We are afraid of being rejected and of being hurt. We are too focused on the every day events of our lives and our relationships with people. Open our eyes to the true needs of the people around us. Their relationship with You is life-changing. Let us put aside our own wants, needs and desires and look to You. You are almighty, You are everlasting, You are eternal, You are real, and You are truly amazing. You give us strength when we are weak. You guide and lead us when we are lost. You are our Creator and our Savior. You are the most important part of our life, why are we so unwillingly to share Your love with others? Give us boldness and courage. Give us the words to say. Use us and our lives to proclaim Your blessings to others. As we praise You with our lives and our hearts, others will see Your love in us. May Your will be done in our lives and be reflected within us. We ask this in the name of Jesus, our Lord and Savior. Amen.

Digging Deeper: Consider a time when you had the courage to share your faith and convictions with someone around you. How was the Lord's presence working through you?

_____

_____

_____

_____

Day 143

But may the righteous be glad and rejoice before God; may they be happy and joyful. Sing to God, sing praise to his name, extol him who rides on the clouds—his name is the Lord—and rejoice before him. A father to the fatherless, a defender of widows, is God in his holy dwelling.

Psalm 68:3-5

Dear Lord,

Our lives on this earth may be difficult, but all things are possible with You. You sustain us and give us hope for each day. You provide for our needs, and You bless us abundantly. We do not need to complain and to worry, for You are with us always. We should be happy and joyful and allow Your love to shine in our lives. We need to be an example for You. We should sing praises and rejoice in Your goodness. Without You, we have nothing. But with You, we have everything. We have help and encouragement for each day. We have hope for our future and we have the promises that You have given us in Your Word. You have not left us alone. You have promised to be with us forever.

God, You care about each one of Your children. You love the little children. You want to be their Father and provide for their needs. You want us to take care of the orphans and the widows and share Your love and blessings with them. You don't want to see people alone and suffering. You have given us families and friends to help us along life's way. You are not a far away God who has created this world and left us on our own. You are a personal God who cares about every aspect of our lives. Help us to praise You in good times and in bad. Help us to trust You when things are going well and when times are hard. Help us to draw near to You and open our hearts to You. You already know everything there is to know about each of us; we can't hide anything from You. Help us to be authentic Christians and to be open and honest, loving and caring. Help us to be more like You and to desire the things that You desire. Open our hearts to Your Word and speak to us. We ask this in the name of Jesus, our Savior, our Lord, our perfect example who is worthy of our love and praise. Amen.

Digging Deeper: God has called us to defend the weak, watch over the widows, share with the poor, and give to others the blessings that we have been given. How have you answered the call to "live your faith" and lovingly meet the needs of others? What is God calling you to do?

_____

_____

_____

_____

Day 144

Praise be to the Lord, to God our Savior, who daily bears our burdens. Our God is a God who saves; from the Sovereign Lord comes escape from death. Surely God will crush the heads of his enemies, the hairy crowns of those who go on in their sins.

Psalm 68:19-21

Dear Lord,

Thank you for bearing our burdens and carrying the loads that weigh us down and are too heavy for us to endure. You understand what our lives are like. You left the splendor and majesty of heaven to live on this earth. You left paradise to humbly come to this world. You came because we needed a Savior. You came to show us how to live. You came to suffer and die for us. You should have been worshiped and adored, but You were mocked and persecuted. You should have been praised and glorified; instead You were beaten and abused. Yet You endured it all. You willingly gave Your life for us. You prayed that God's will would be done, and You lovingly followed the difficult path to the cross. You were faithful and You trusted in Your Father.

Lord, we need to learn from Your example. We need to trust in the perfect plan of our Heavenly Father. We need to come before Him in prayer and lay down our burdens. We need to surrender ourselves and our selfish desires and seek His will for our lives. We need to believe and not be filled with doubts and questions. We need to follow and not try to make our own plans. We need to trust that God knows all things and He certainly knows what is best for us. Thank you for saving us, for reaching down and touching our lives. You have given us faith and hope. You have given us a reason for living. You have filled our lives with meaning and purpose. Yet sometimes we want our own way. We want to be in control. We are selfish, and we are sinful. We need forgiveness, and we need Your guidance. We need to be saved from ourselves. Show us the way, the truth, and the life that we should live. Teach us to trust in You completely and allow You to work in our lives. We can't save ourselves. We need a Savior. We need You, Jesus, today, tomorrow, and always. Be our shepherd and show us the way. In Your precious name, we pray. Amen.

Digging Deeper: God gives us our daily bread and daily bears our burdens. In what ways has He provided for you? How does He meet your needs?

_____

_____

_____

Day 145

Sing to God, O kingdoms of the earth, sing praise to the Lord, to him who rides the ancient skies above, who thunders with mighty voice. Proclaim the power of God, whose majesty is over Israel, whose power is in the skies. You are awesome, O God, in your sanctuary; the God of Israel gives power and strength to his people.

Psalm 68:32-35

Dear God,

You are glorious and majestic. You are so powerful and mighty. You are awesome and amazing. You are holy and just. You are righteous and perfect in every way. You are worthy of our love, thanks, and praise. Your power is proclaimed throughout creation and throughout the universe. The heavens declare Your righteousness. The skies shine forth Your glory. We are in awe of Your holiness and humbled in Your presence. You are almighty, and yet You care about us, Your lowly creation. You take the time to listen to our prayers as we bow down before Your holy throne. We seek Your shelter and Your sanctuary. We desire a safe haven from the cares and concerns of this world. We want to get away from the pressure, the problems, and the burdens of this world. We turn to You, our Father, for strength and guidance. We long to be comforted by You and have our hearts renewed and our faith restored. Your voice thunders through the skies, but it also whispers to us in the quietness of our souls. Help us to be still and to seek Your presence. Comfort us during our times of great need when our sorrows and sadness are overwhelming. Help us when we can no longer help ourselves. Lead us when we do not have the courage to continue on our own. Help us to trust in You and to seek Your wisdom. You alone are God. You alone are worthy of our praise, our hearts, our souls, and our lives. Help us to praise You with our entire being. Help us to seek You first in our lives. Help us to draw near to You and spend quality time with You each day.

As we sing Your praises and worship You, let us proclaim Your majesty to the world. Let us lift our voices to You and share the faith You have given to us. Let us love You with our inmost being and serve You with our lives. You are the God of Israel and the Lord of my life. I am blessed and privileged to know You and I humbly seek Your presence. Fill my life with Your love and kindness and wash me clean of my sins and selfishness. Create in me a pure heart. I ask all these things in the precious name of Your Son, my Savior. Amen.

Digging Deeper: What are some ways that you can seek the Lord first in your life? What things in your life or what parts of your life should you change?

_____

_____

_____

_____

Day 146

Save me, O God, for the waters have come up to my neck. I sink in the miry depths, where there is no foothold. I have come into the deep waters; the floods engulf me. I am worn out calling for help; my throat is parched. My eyes fail, looking for my God.

Psalm 69:1-3

Dear God,

I am sinking. I am overwhelmed. I am lost. I am barely holding on. My strength is gone. My burdens are great. My troubles are many. I am tired. I cannot hold on much longer. Everything is too hard for me. I am having a hard time making it through each day. I am weary. I am worried. I am exhausted!

Lord, You are my source of strength. You are always there to hear my cries for help. You listen to my prayers. Your love for me is unconditional. You have promised to be with me now and forever. You can do all things. You are in control. You have promised to carry my burden and lighten my load. You have the answers to the questions I have yet to ask. You know what is right and what is best for me. Why do I suffer? Why do I wait to come to You? Why am I so stubborn? Why do I try to do everything on my own? Why don't I seek You first?

Lord, I need You. I need Your tender mercy. I need Your lovingkindness. I need Your forgiveness. I need to be comforted by Your loving arms. I need Your support and Your strength. I need to believe in You and humbly come before You. You are my God, and You are my life. You have given so much to me and blessed me beyond my wildest dreams. Help me to always keep my eyes focused on You. Help me not to be distracted by the problems, troubles, and trials of this world. Help me to remember that I am Your precious child and You care about me. Help my unbelief and calm my fears. Surround me with Your love and show me the way. I look to You for healing and for help. I lift up all these requests in the name of Jesus who can do all things. Amen.

Digging Deeper: What wears you out? How does God's strength change your life on a daily basis?

_____

_____

_____

_____

Day 147

May those who hope in you not be disgraced because of me, O Lord, the Lord Almighty; may those who seek you not be put to shame because of me, O God of Israel. For I endure scorn for your sake, and shame covers my face. But I pray to you, O Lord, in the time of your favor; in your great love, O God, answer me with your sure salvation.

Psalm 69:6-7, 13

Dear Lord,

I want to live my life as an example for others. I want my love for You to shine through and touch the lives of those around me. I want Your name to be worshiped and praised. But sometimes I fail! I am afraid that I am disgracing Your name. I look like a hypocrite because I say one thing and do another. I want people to be drawn closer to You and not be "turned off" by my life and my example. I am sinful. I make mistakes. I am not perfect, not even close. I don't do the things that I should do, and I do things that I shouldn't do. I am a work in progress. I pray that You would not give up on me. I pray that You would continue to work in my heart and in my life. Help me to be more like You and to desire the things that You desire. Help me to keep my eyes focused more on You and less on me.

Lord, You alone are perfect. I need You and I need Your forgiveness. You surround me with Your love and fill me with peace and hope. Everything I have comes from You. You are the most important part of my life. When I am down, pick me up and show me Your plan and Your will for my life. When I am feeling guilty, take away my sin and cleanse my heart and my soul. Only You can provide true forgiveness and make me whole. When I have hurt someone or offended someone, show me how to repair the relationship and restore communication. When I am hurting, send Your Holy Spirit to comfort me. In my weakness, Your love can show through and Your name can be praised. For when I am weak, You are strong. I know that my strength comes from You. Thank you for never giving up on me! Thank you for covering me with Your righteousness and forgiveness. Thank you for listening to my prayers. Thank you for loving me. In Your name, dear Jesus, I pray. Amen.

Digging Deeper: Think of a time when God shined through your weakness. Were you able to share the source of your strength with others? Was your faith strengthened by God's almighty power?

_____

_____

_____

_____

Day 148

Answer me, O Lord, out of the goodness of your love; in your great mercy turn to me. Do not hide your face from your servant; answer me quickly, for I am in trouble. Come near and rescue me; redeem me because of my foes. You know how I am scorned, disgraced and shamed; all my enemies are before you.

Psalm 69:16-19

Dear Lord,

When the world seems to be winning and my life is spinning out of control, be my peace. When I can't see past the next few minutes, bring calm and understanding in my life. When the problems and troubles, the "red tape" and the bureaucracy of the world are sapping my energy and depleting my strength, speak to my heart and renew me. When it seems my enemies are in control and You are far away, draw near to me. Help me to remember that You have defeated this world, sin, death, and the devil. These things have no real power over me. You are in control. I need to spend time with You and to read Your Word and seek Your will. You have the answers that I need to hear. You know the questions that are in my heart. You know what I need and what is best for me. I am lost in this world because heaven is my true home. I don't understand all the ways of this world. Many things don't make sense to me. I need Your guidance. Send Your Holy Spirit to show me the way, the truth and the life. Help me not to get tangled up in sin and overwhelmed by the ways of this world. Transform me. Create in me a clean, pure, open, honest heart that reflects Your love. Rescue me. Surround me with Your loving-kindness and renew my faith. Redeem me. Help me to see Your hand in my life and to remember that there is more to this life than what I can see. Forgive me. Take away my pride and my selfishness. Take away my need to control all things. Help me to surrender to Your will and Your ways and to trust in You completely. Sometimes my head knows the answers, but my heart wants to worry. Sometimes I want to trust in You and believe what You say, but the distractions of the world draw me away from You.

Lord, thank you for never giving up on me. Thank you for touching my heart and changing my life. Thank you for Your promise to always be with me. Thank you for Your life on earth and Your death on the cross. Thank you for Your holy Word and for speaking to me. Please calm my heart and answer my prayers today and always. In Your precious name, I pray. Amen.

Digging Deeper: How do you give control of your life to God? How can you commit your life, your heart, your soul and your mind to Him? What problems in this world cause you to lose control?

Day 149

I am in pain and distress; may your salvation, O God, protect me. I will praise God's name in song and glorify him with thanksgiving. This will please the Lord more than an ox, more than a bull with its horns and hoofs. The poor will see and be glad—you who seek God, may Your hearts live.

Psalm 69:29-32

Dear God,

I am suffering. I am hurting and my heart is heavy. I need You in my life, and I need Your comfort and Your strength. Some days are very hard. Some challenges seem too difficult for me. Some problems seem overwhelming. Sometimes everything seems impossible and I do not have the strength to endure. You, O God, my Father can carry me through these painful times. You have shown me the way, and You can guide me through this life. Sometimes the road is long and hard, and I can't see the light at the end of the tunnel. Some days I can barely find the strength to get out of bed. Some challenges seem too difficult to even begin. But You, O Lord, have promised to be with me always. I am never truly alone, and I am not on my own. In You, I find hope. In You, I find strength. In You, I find comfort. You are my Father, You created me, You know me completely, and You love me unconditionally. Although I often disappoint You, You forgive me. Although I fall short of Your perfect standard, You never turn away from me or reject me. When I ask Your forgiveness, You wipe my slate clean and allow me a fresh start. When I feel that I can no longer go on, You speak to me in a still, small voice and give me the confidence and ability to try. When I am in pain, You comfort me and take care of me.

Lord, without You I could not endure the trials and temptations of this world. I would be broken and lost, and my suffering would be great. But You are faithful! When I seek You and humbly come before You, You accept me for who I am. You lift me up and carry me. You alone are worthy of praise. I am so thankful that I can come to You in prayer and lift up my hearts desires. I need Your love, Your acceptance, Your forgiveness, and Your strength. You know my heart and my needs. Help me to worship You and love You. To obey is better than sacrifice. My love, my life, my heart, and my soul mean more to You than any sacrifices. You, Lord, are the perfect sacrifice. You gave Your life for me. To You, be all praise and glory now and forevermore. In Your name I pray. Amen.

Digging Deeper: What does it mean "to obey is better than sacrifice"? When is it difficult for you to obey God? What sacrifices have you made for God, and what sacrifices has He made for you? How do they compare?

_____

_____

_____

_____

Day 150

Hasten, O God, to save me; O Lord, come quickly to help me. May those who seek my life be put to shame and confusion; may all who desire my ruin be turned back in disgrace. But may all who seek you rejoice and be glad in You; may those who love your salvation always say, "Let God be exalted!"

Psalm 70:1-2, 4

Dear God,

I know that whenever I call, You hear me. You listen to me. You answer me. You love me. Sometimes it seems like my enemies are winning the battle and I will not survive. But in my heart I know the truth. I know Your truth. You are the Almighty God, the master of the universe, the Creator of the world, and the Lord of my life. I want to praise Your name and rejoice in You. I want to draw near to You and to seek Your face. I want to humbly come before You, to be still and know that You are God. I want my life to count for You. I want to follow Your ways and seek Your will for my life. I don't want to be swallowed up by the enemy. I want to live for You and shine Your light into this darkened world. I want to make a difference and see other people come to know You and praise Your holy name. I want people to know who You are and what You have done in my life.

But, Lord, sometimes I am frightened, and I am weak. I am confused, and I am filled with questions and with doubts. Sometimes

I am lost, and I feel alone. I know that You will take care of me. I know that I am never truly alone, but sometimes I need to be reminded of Your love. I need boldness and courage to share my faith. I need to put aside my wants, needs, and desires and look to see how I can serve others and serve You. My family and friends need to know You, and I pray they will see You working in my life and changing my heart. Maybe they will see how You answer my prayers and provide for my needs. I need to trust in You completely. I need to let Your love shine through me. I need to share the many blessings that I have been given with those around me. I need You and Your healing touch. I need Your guidance and Your strength. You are my amazing, incredible Heavenly Father, and I am thankful for You. Please answer my prayers according to Your will. In Jesus' name I pray. Amen.

Digging Deeper: How do you make your life count for God? How has God blessed you? For what blessings do you give Him praise?

_____

_____

_____

_____

WORDS FOR
EVERYDAY LIVING

Shelter me from the storms of life. You are my refuge. Lift me out of the pit. Show me the way, Your perfect way that I might follow. Lead me beside the still waters, and quiet the winds and the waves that threaten me.

Be my light and my guide through this crazy, busy, stress-filled, yet wonderful world. Help me to keep my eyes focused on You and to trust in You completely. Help my unbelief and restore my faith. Answer the questions that are in my heart, and draw me close to You.

I am the clay, and You are the potter. You shaped me and formed me, and You continue to work in and through my life. You provide me with all that I need in this world.

Although my enemies conspire against me and look for ways to bring me down, You are always there to build me up and encourage me. In You, I can do all things. In You, I have power and strength and courage. In You, I have hope.

Our hearts and our lives need to be cleansed. We need You because we can't make it on our own. We try our best, but it isn't good enough. Our motives aren't pure. Our actions are not holy. We deceive others, and we even deceive ourselves.

You are to be worshiped and praised now and forevermore. Thank you for creating us and for changing our lives with Your love. Thank you for listening to our prayers and for teaching us how to love. Forgive us for the chaos that we create and give us Your perfect peace.

As we think about how awesome You are and how wonderful and powerful You are, give us the courage to talk with others about You. And help us to always sing joyfully and lovingly share our faith with our lips, our voices, our hearts and our lives. Blessed are we because You have chosen us.

When we are lonely, You lovingly wrap Your arms around us and remind us that we are special to You and we are Your children. When we feel worthless, You remind us that we were chosen and called by You and we are precious in Your sight.

Thank you for never giving up on me. Although I have doubts, You are always faithful. Although I deserve punishment, You give me mercy and love. Although I have turned away from You and have followed my own desires, You forgive me and gently lead me back into Your loving arms.

Help us to be authentic Christians and to be open and honest, loving and caring. Help us to be more like You and to desire the things that You desire. Open our hearts to Your Word and speak to us.

Lord, we need to learn from Your example. We need to trust in the perfect plan of our Heavenly Father. We need to come before Him in prayer and lay down our burdens. We need to surrender ourselves and our selfish desires and seek His will for our lives.

We want to get away from the pressure, the problems, and the burdens of this world. We turn to You, our Father, for strength and guidance. We long to be comforted by You and have our hearts renewed and our faith restored. Your voice thunders through the skies, but it also whispers to us in the quietness of our souls.

You are my God, and You are my life. You have given so much to me and blessed me beyond my wildest dreams. Help me to always keep my eyes focused on You. Help me not to be distracted by the problems, troubles, and trials of this world. Help me to remember that I am Your precious child and You care about me.

You are the most important part of my life. When I am down, pick me up and show me Your plan and Your will for my life. When I am feeling guilty, take away my sin and cleanse my heart and my soul. Only You can provide true forgiveness and make me whole.

Create in me a clean, pure, open, honest heart that reflects Your love. Rescue me. Surround me with Your loving kindness and renew my faith. Redeem me. Help me to see Your hand in my life and to remember that there is more to this life than what I can see.

To obey is better than sacrifice. My love, my life, my heart, and my soul mean more to You than any sacrifices. You, Lord, are the perfect sacrifice. You gave Your life for me.

Sometimes it seems like my enemies are winning the battle and I will not survive. But in my heart I know the truth. I know Your truth. You are the Almighty God, the master of the universe, the Creator of the world, and the Lord of my life.